WAY o

Palmistry

WAY *of*
Palmistry

Lilian Verner-Bonds

Thorsons

Thorsons
An Imprint of HarperCollins*Publishers*
77–85 Fulham Palace Road
Hammersmith, London W6 8JB

The Thorsons website address is: www.thorsons.com

and *Thorsons*
are trademarks of HarperCollins*Publishers* Limited

First published by HarperCollins*Publishers* 1997
This edition published by *Thorsons* 2002

3 5 7 9 10 8 6 4 2

A catalogue record for this book
is available from the British Library

ISBN 0 00 712008 7

Printed and bound in Great Britain by
Martins The Printers Limited, Berwick upon Tweed

Contents

Dedicated to my daughter,
Louise Jane Verner
The Joy and Light of my Life

Acknowledgements

I would like to express my thanks to my editor, Dr Ronald L. Bonewitz, and to the memory of my geriatric cat, Sullivan, who spent his last six months sitting beside me as I wrote this book.

Introduction

The hand is the organ of organs, the instrument
of instruments.   *Aristotle*

Palm reading is a personal experience – it does not concern itself
with the weather, world events, or the state of the economy! Each
hand is unique to the individual, and gives a step-by-step account of
the individual's life, from birth to death; it is a *life-recorder*. As our
luck, fortune or destiny can change, so too can the lines and markings on our hands.

Our hands link the intentions of our heart with the reasoning of our
mind. When we become aware of their unconscious language and
recorded messages, we begin to have totally fresh sources of information yielding new insights about ourselves.

In the hands are patterns of power. Understanding the messages in
our palms we become much less the victims of circumstance. The
hands build up a picture of the psyche, the inner needs and wants,
as distinct from mere fortune telling. Our health, diet and the daily
toll of living are also recorded. The inner perspectives available can
shed much light on issues and difficulties encountered in daily life.

Hands can be read in two completely different ways. A *psychic* hand
reader may not have memorized the meanings of every single line
and marking on the hand. For them the hand becomes a point of
focus, a pattern on which to 'tune in'. The *scientific* hand reader uses
the meanings of all the features presented in the hand so that a picture can be built up from the shapes and meanings alone. Whether
you are psychic or not, it is important to get a solid basic grounding
in palmistry to always ensure that you are on the right track, and
correctly reading the information presented to you in the hands.

Always remember that nothing is fixed. We always have the chance to change if we want to. Action brings about change and action is the word given in ancient sanskrit texts to explain Karma, which is our path in life. This is governed according to what we were before we are born into this life, and its connection to how we live this life and move forward into the next. Everything moves in life; nothing stands still. Part of being alive now is to see how we conduct ourselves, whether we take hold of the rudder which steers our opportunities or setbacks, or whether we float along blinkered against events that are happening to us; in other words, always the effect of other people's cause. We have the gift of free will which enables us to have a degree of control over what happens to us. If we had no say about the direction of our lives, then there would be no point in being alive as we would be unable to grow and learn.

Our state of mind can turn around almost any course we have set in life, bringing in the Health, Wealth and Happiness we desire. In reading the message our handprint gives us and taking the necessary steps, we can become master of our own destiny.

As you undertake this study of palmistry, you are following in the footsteps of the ancients. Palmistry, more properly called Chiromancy (from the Greek word *Cheir*, hand), was practised in the Orient some fifty centuries ago. Ancient Asian and Chinese hand reading techniques practised 3,000 years ago are still used in present-day reading. The Greeks held it in high repute and classical literature, in particular the works of Aristotle (384-322BC) are full of references to divination by means of the hands. Yet its origins go back even further – prehistoric carvings and paintings of hands were created to demonstrate the hand's superiority over other parts of the body. Indeed, it became a symbol of man's mastery. To this day in the east it is extensively practised – in India, China, Syria and Egypt.

We should expect an art with such ancient lineage to possess a well-established basis of rules and procedures, and this is true of palmistry. It was formulated centuries ago, and medieval writers on the subject are numerous. It is suggested that the Romany people, who learned palmistry from Arab sources, brought the art from the east into the west.

One of the earliest printed books is a German treatise on Chiromancy by Martlieb (1448). Another remarkable book on the subject was written by Cocles in 1504. In the next few hundred years the art of palmistry was recorded by the French, Germans and Italians.

For nearly two centuries palmistry declined, but in the middle of the nineteenth century two energetic French investigators, d'Arpentigny and Desbarrolles, resuscitated it. The former was concerned mainly with chirognomy, or discerning the character by the shape and form of the hands, and the latter founded the art of chiromancy, or divination by the lines of the hand.

The hands are the mirror of your soul; they will tell you about *you*. The lines start to develop about thirteen to seventeen weeks after conception as a foetus in the womb. By the time you are born you bring with you a map of yourself in your hands. I am often asked to read new-born baby's hands within 48 hours of birth, so that an understanding can be gained about future health and well-being from the child's personal chart that is recorded in their palms.

The study of palmistry can be overwhelming: 'I would love to be able to read hands, but all the books I've read are far too complicated. I've given up after a while because it is so frustrating trying to get to grips with complicated and conflicting diagrams and texts.'

This is the type of comment that I've heard so often from people who are interested in learning the language of the hands. In fact, learning the basic map of the hands can be *simple*, and that's what this book will show you.

I have been asked: 'Do I have to be psychic to read the hands?' The answer is, you already are! Everyone has within them the ability to draw upon that sensitive side of themselves, and palmistry is the classic method that enables you to do this.

The Romany people that brought palmistry from the east to the west certainly did not need to go into great study worthy of a degree; but they still had basic rules to follow, and these I'm going to give to you. The art of palmistry is vast and there are so many techniques that can be employed. There is so much to remember. That is why a system helps.

Take it step by step, line by line! Slowly, and cautiously. A basic structured reading is easier both to give and to receive. Random readings by beginners prove misleading. If you are willing to follow this simple system, you will become a good palmist and be able to enhance your life, and that of your family and friends, with wisdom and joy.

This book is designed to accommodate all degrees of interest in palmistry: from those who only wish to do a minimal reading, enough to entertain friends at parties, to those who intend to make it a serious study. The beauty of the system is that if you choose to learn to read in stages, from the simplest reading to the most complex, what you have learned to do in the last reading becomes the foundation for the next. To do a full palmistry reading to the highest degree of accuracy requires you to integrate many factors, a skill that will come only with *practice*.

NOTE: This book assumes that its reader will be using the information herein to develop their own skills as a palmist. Therefore where a description occurs of the aspects or traits associated with a particular feature, it always addresses the person whose hand is being read as 'they'. For example, 'they will have a tendency to over-indulgence'. The 'they' in each instance, is the person for whom the reader is doing a palm reading. The same information applies, of course, to the reader himself or herself if they are reading their own palm.

The chapters are arranged in the order that a palmist examines the various features of the hands in a full reading. Because there is a certain amount of cross-checking between various features, from time to time the book will refer the reader to material in a later chapter. This, however, has been kept to an absolute minimum.

ONE

GETTING

Started

When you embark on reading a palm, it's best to clear your mind so that you can absorb anything you desire. Remember, intuitively, you can do it anyway.

Palmistry is the only complete form of self-knowledge that doesn't require you to purchase any props, other than your own or someone else's hands.

Don't be afraid to 'feel' the hands at first, closing your eyes if you wish. This is part of 'tuning in' and preparing yourself to interpret what you receive when reading the palms.

Start with you own palms and find the line, shape, or marking you have chosen to work on, and then read up on it in the book. Try to match it to something the book is telling you – eventually a pattern will emerge.

Don't jump around the palm from one line or place to another, although it's tempting. You'll eventually get on faster if you stick to one line or part at first: understand all of its intricacies; become a master of one line or section at a time, rather than master of none.

General Advice to the Beginner

- Be patient
- Proceed step-by-step
- Be realistic about how much you know
- Don't do casual or random readings

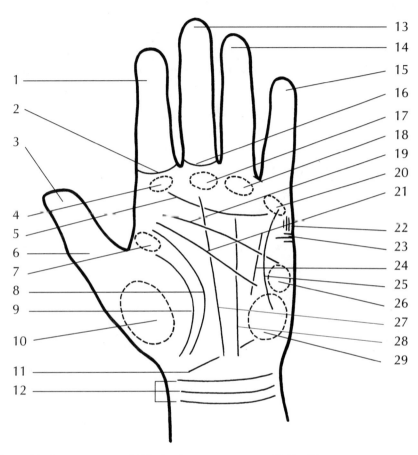

1 Finger of Jupiter	11 Via Lasciva	21 Headline
2 Solomon's ring	12 Rascettes/Bracelets	22 Child lines
3 Phalange of will	13 Finger of Saturn	23 Line of marriage
4 Mount of Jupiter	14 Finger of Apollo	24 Mercury line/liver line
5 Girdle of Venus	15 Finger of Mercury	25 Line of intuition
6 Phalange of logic	16 Ring of Saturn	26 Upper mount of Mars
7 Lower mount of Mars	17 Mount of Saturn	27 Line of fate
8 Lifeline	18 Mount of Apollo	28 Line of the sun
9 Line of Mars	19 Heartline	29 Mount of the moon
10 Mount of Venus	20 Mount of Mercury	

Figure 1: The Basic Map of the Hand

Seating

I recommend that the palmist and the client sit more or less side-by-side; not uncomfortably close (especially for the client), but close enough that the client's palm, when resting, can easily be read in a close to upright position. You should not have to try to read a hand upside down or sideways!

The Best Time of the Day for Reading

There is no specific time of day that is best for reading, although in Asia they advocate reading at around sunrise because they believe that the blood is stronger in the extremities of the body at that time. I feel that it is best to do a reading when the person has been up a few hours, as this allows the colourings in the palms to become stronger. If a person has a tendency towards low blood pressure, the hands can appear very pale until the metabolism speeds up. You can always press the section in question and let go, so that the blood flows back into the lines, markings, etc. There are prominent colour meanings attached to various lines and marks, and this will bring them out more distinctly.

Yes or No

When a person asks questions like 'Shall I be happy?, or 'Will I find someone?', unless you are a very advanced palmist, do *not* answer yes or no if in doubt. It is better to explain to the client how they may best achieve the satisfaction they desire through the positive indications on the hand. But use only the ones you are sure about!

Distressed Client

If a person seems upset and anxious, try to emphasize and direct them to the positive markings present. The person in a distressed mental state will not be in a position to change the negative traits. Always encourage them to improve on the positive aspects, which will in turn affect and help to overcome adversity.

Health

In health matters, first of all look for a positive Life Line, which will show a fortunate set of circumstances and opportunities. A strong Head Line is a good backup to the Life Line, adding the dimension of 'mind over matter'. Look also for the absence of a Mercury Line, which is a very positive sign. Additionally, the nails and their colour are good indicators for health.

If the person is lacking in positive health indicators, it suggests that rather than bad health per se, the person will just need to make an extra effort in caring for themselves. **Word of warning:** Do not give medical advice.

Conflicting Markings

When both of the palm's markings and shapes seem to offer con-flicting outcomes, then it is best *not to guess* what the outcome will be. If in doubt, say nothing! The mere fact that there is confusion shown usually means that *neither* will happen, or that something totally dif-ferent will be coming into their lives later. Unless you are a psychic and can foresee the future, it's best not to commit when it is *not* clear.

Prediction

Although there are no absolute guarantees when predicting the future from the hands, nonetheless they can indicate what might occur or is likely to occur. The benefit of 'far seeing' through palmistry is that steps can be taken to correct what may be indicated by any adverse markings. This means that we do not have to remain a victim to the future!

Words of Advice

- Be tactful.
- Be grounded yourself so that you do not become carried away by what you unfold.
- Be a clear communicator.
- Be as objective as possible.
- Never use a reading to gain control over another person, or to impress them.

> Palmistry is a very intimate exchange between two people. Treat it delicately, and with respect and compassion for the client.

- *Always* remember what it is like to be on the receiving end.
- *Always* work ahead. Whatever the client tells you, make sure you are moving on to gather more information.

Reading the hand of another person is a very serious matter, and it involves tremendous responsibility. Whilst it is comfortable to focus on the positive aspects when dealing with a client we should also keep to mind the negative areas as well.

Good palmists rarely make sweeping statements. What you can achieve when *all* the details are collected is a pattern and a set of tendencies or indications, with nothing fixed. Fate and destiny are not set, and you will always find a mix of good and bad.

The Types of Readings

The Short Reading only requires you to learn the meanings of the Lines (Chapters 9–14). This short beginner's reading, although limiting, will be nonetheless accurate in the information it provides. Understanding the lines is basic to all readings, and it will provide a short, quick, very general understanding of the person's past, present and future. The palmist opting for the Short Reading must understand that there are many other factors and influences indicated in the remainder of the hand. When added, these other factors will give a fuller understanding, which can modify the meanings of the Lines when read only by themselves.

The Medium Reading adds the Shape of the Hands (Chapter 2) and the Finger Nails (Chapter 6) to the previously learned material on the Lines. At this point the new palmist must begin to make decisions regarding the prominence to be given to the differing information provided from the additional sources. The new palmist's intuitive talents begin to come into play here as well, talents that will be exercised further in the next stage, the complete reading.

WAY of

The Complete Reading: Practice from the earlier readings will aid the serious palmist in linking, integrating and interpreting the wealth of information available in the entire hand.

Both you and your clients will be astonished at the accuracy of the results.

TWO

THE

Hands

The Right Hand and the Left Hand

To begin, it is necessary to establish which hand is which; which hand represents the past or potential, and which is the hand of now and the future. Generally in palmistry when a person is right-handed the left hand is regarded as the hand we are born with and the right hand is how we make out in life with the opportunities and possible setbacks that we are handed. The original understanding that the left hand was the one to work with, indicating the future, was because it was closest to the heart. This came about because the heart was considered to be the prime organ within the human body. It was believed to record man's very thoughts and feelings.

Later on, the left hand was viewed with superstition for hundreds of years in some cultures. It was considered the hand of the devil whereas the right, which was offered in greetings, was regarded as the hand of honesty.

When giving a reading, just ask your client if they are right handed or left handed. You will be surprised how many use both hands equally, and thus don't know. A simple test will establish the most prominent, active hand, by clasping their hands alternately, as if for a handshake. The hand which grips yours the most powerfully is their active hand, the dominant hand of now, the hand which reveals incoming events. Normally when a person is right handed that will be the hand of now and the future.

The weaker of the two represents the past.

The Left Hand – One's Potential

The left hand denotes inherited traits from past lives and pre-birth conditions giving information on our possibilities – what we have come into this life with. Here the potential future talents and abilities will be revealed. A person should not despair if any seemingly extreme traits and marks appear, as changes along the way are possible, which can be seen on the other hand. If the hand seems a little bare and looks like there is not much indicated for the future, realize that the person will probably be a late developer. Compare it to the other palm for information regarding what is happening now and what could be coming in. It may be full of life's rich events which means they will not get started into life's positive pattern of events until later than most. The left hand also symbolizes the subconscious.

The Right Hand – Now and the Future

The right hand is the working hand of Now and what is coming in until the day they pass on. This is where the much-desired ability of divination or fortune telling comes in. We may find that the hand of potential has indicated certain possibilities for the person, only to find that on the 'working hand of now' – the other hand – these do not show up. They have not materialized. The indication was there for the person but they have not taken it up or followed it through. You may also find on the right hand that there are events indicated for the future but they were not recorded in the left hand of potential. This shows that the person has acquired these traits and created opportunities for themselves as they have progressed in life.

The right hand also symbolizes the conscious mind.

Hand Shapes

The basic overall shape of the hands indicates the underlying disposition of the person concerned. The basic shape of the hands reflects the individual's core qualities. There are positive and negative traits which we all have – each shape reveals these traits. The art is to recognize and promote the positive whilst at the same time finding ways to integrate the negative areas. To find a balance is the key. The shape of the hand gives valuable information regarding the pleasures that we have and the pitfalls. They are an instant visual indicator of the 'have' and 'have not' aspects that we possess. There are two basic hand shapes that the other five shapes are variations of:

1.   *The Square, which is the down-to-earth shape.*
2.   *The Conic, which is round and creative.*

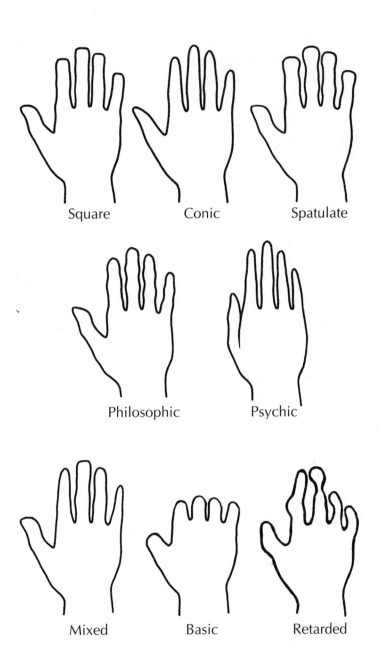

Figure 2: Hand and Fingertip Shapes

Always take into account the shape of the fingertips in deciding the hand shape. The five variants are the Spatulate, the Psychic, the Philosophical, the Mixed and the Basic. The study of the hand shapes and fingers is called Cheirognomy, *cheir* being the Greek word for the hand. It deals with the character of the owner. The hand shape is the container for the rest of palmistry. It can be regarded as the cover of life's book.

Sometimes a person can have one hand belonging to one shape and the other hand will be another shape. This is rare, but if so just read each hand for what it is. If the hands are different shapes, according to which hand it is, it will show that the person has either gained or lost something. For example, if the left hand of potential is a Psychic shape, and the active hand of now has a square, down-to-earth hand shape, then it shows that the psychic ability from childhood has been lost as an adult.

When reading a palm always refer back to the shape of the hand, which sets the tone for the whole reading. It gives you your first clue when coming to an understanding. Certain shapes also suggest the different kinds of careers and occupations that would be best suited for that person.

The Square Hand – Down to Earth

The square hand literally has square fingertips and a square look about it, usually on a short fairly squat palm. The wrist will be thick. The characteristics are practicality and conventionality.

A useful hand. The subjects of a square-hand can turn their hands to anything. They are the salt of the earth. Industry, business and commerce are suited to them because they have methodical minds and keep to the rules. Stubbornness and patience also prevail with a dislike of emotional public displays. They are not drawn to music and the arts, and will not believe what they do not understand. They can be quite rigid and unyielding but are full of integrity and always carry out their promises.

The Conic Hand – Creative and Artistic

The conic hand is the artistic hand. The palm will be longer and more slender than the square hand and the finger tips will be rounded. There is a restlessness about the personality, forever seeking stimulating challenges. Quite often a problematical love life. They never stand still long enough to gather any roots. Personal comforts are a priority but they can be generous if the mood takes them. They are extremely creative and love the arts. They would rather work for the love of it than for money. Working from instinct and impulse comes naturally to them. Patience is not one of their virtues, so it's not always easy to finish projects. They can be social climbers. They respond to sympathetic influences and are inclined to be up in the clouds one minute and down in the dumps the next. Drawn to leading a public life. Work very well in any profession where there is people interaction.

The Spatulate Hand – Action and Inventiveness

The shape of a spatulate hand can be recognized by the spreading out of the end of the finger tips like a fan. The rest of the hand can be a mixture of the square and conic shape. Extremely unconventional in their thinking and ways of behaviour. Very quick-witted and fast to act. Grass doesn't grow under their feet, which can make them a little difficult to keep up with. They can be great fun to be around as they are stimulating, self-confident and resourceful. Forever seeking an answer, they are original and inventive. An independent spirit, they do not take kindly to a mundane job from nine to five. Excellent as mechanics and engineers, in fact any profession

15

can appeal to them. They often bring about change whatever career they decide to follow – having a great flare for the new they are always eager to explore new paths.

The Psychic Hand – Imagination and the Medium

The psychic hand as recorded from earliest palmistry is said to be the most beautiful hand shape of them all. It is extremely rare to find a truly psychic shape in the western world; you will find most of them in Asia. The finger tips will be long and pointed, tapering to almost nothing. The rest of the hand will be small and slender and extremely delicate. It is called a psychic hand because the tips of the fingers are able to receive energy impulses from the atmosphere. The pointed tip picks up the vibration which can quickly pass on down into the hand. A square-tipped finger almost stops easy access for this kind of intuitive flow. Rather inclined to idealism, they have difficulty surviving in the real world as they are not programmed to deal with the nitty gritty. They have a need to be looked after as they can be easily duped because they trust too much. It is hard to judge them by ordinary standards. Provided they are protected by the shrewd and strong they can capitalize on their sensitive natures through their intuitive gifts which have the ability to pierce the veil of the future. All forms of the mystic arts attract them as their imagination is ever awake.

The Philosophic Hand – Studious and Level Headed

The philosophical hand is easily recognized by its long angular shape with bony fingers. The fingertips are usually long and round with a slight saucer shape, a combination of the two. The main characteristic sign of this shaped hand are the knotted large knuckles.

Possessing this type of hand means there is a greater understanding of the world's workings inside and out. These deep thinkers are also proud loners. Crowds do not draw them. As far as success is concerned they have a natural wisdom that unfortunately rarely leads to gold. Great humanists, individualism is their key. The ego is to the fore, regarding themselves a cut above the masses. They love secret societies and anything connected to religion. The East and all its mysteries fascinate them. They are the philosophers and as such can be very thoughtful indeed to their fellow men. They have extreme patience and great tenacity to follow through. The sciences with all their discoveries suit them well. Whatever they choose as a profession they will always think it through.

Mixed Hands – All Sorts

To recognize the mixed-shape hand look to the fingers. They will have a mixture at the fingertips of all or some of the other shapes. The palm could be any shape – square, round, long or short; but the mixed-shaped fingertips govern its character. Great adaptability is always present as they have the ability to bring to the fore any action that is required because they literally have access to various sources of information at their fingertips. Extremely eloquent in speech, they make good diplomats. The media draws them, particularly journalism. They make great gossip columnists. These people rarely suffer at the hands of others as they seem to have a great self-preservation streak. They have an uncanny ability to anticipate happenings and outcomes, which puts them in the position of always being one jump ahead.

The Basic Hand – The Grafter with Limited Prospects

This shape is a short, squat hand with stubby fingers and squarish fingertips. Normally comes from humble stock where manual work was the means of survival. Pomp and circumstance do not impress them even if they are aware of it. Can be crude in their dealings with society. Despite the fact that they can jump from being a pauper to a king they will always revert to their humble beginnings. A millionaire with this shape hand buys antiques because of their monetary value and not because he appreciates their beauty. Can produce dictators, but the broader the palm the less likely the person is to elevate themselves. This shape will either stay uneducated or only climb a few rungs up the social ladder. They often work in jobs that other people don't want to do. This hand was much prized in the days of farming and heavy work when strength was a prime advantage.

The Idiots Hand/The Mentally Retarded

This hand is so ill-shaped that it almost looks deformed. The fingers will be short and crippled and the palms very thick. Usually the half-developed brain and the congenital idiot go hand-in-hand with this shape. The mental degradation indicated by this type means that the person will usually have to be taken care of as they have no concept of the world and its workings.

Hand Size

Regardless of the shape of the hand, its size must be taken into account. The larger it is the more emphasis is given to a particular hand-shape's meaning. The smaller the hand, the less the impact of a shape's meaning.

The Large-Hand Personality

An over-large hand compared to the rest of the body shows that the person has an incredible eye for detail. They are not fooled by the show and glamour of anything. They always read the small print!

The Small-Hand Personality

The small-handed can be bohemian in their outlook – always broad-minded even if a little chaotic in the everyday running of their lives.

Even mundane activities are done with finesse but they are still able to envisage things on a large scale.

The Back of the Hands

It has always been 'cross my palm' and not the 'back of my hand' with silver. Originally the back of the hand or the top was the part that was read alongside the shape of the fingers and nails. This area gives us the persona. It shows the dimension of our personality that we present to the outside world. It was much later that the hand was turned over to reveal the palm, which gives us the inner man and his thoughts which can be read through the lines, markings and mounts.

The back of the hand gives more information than you might think. The texture of the skin in particular can reveal the person's sensitivity, depending on its quality. A smoother-skin will show an easier run in life, using a softer approach. The coarser the skin is, the harsher the personality and the tougher one is in dealing with life's ups and downs. Also revealing are the finger's shape, knuckles, hair and nails, as the following chapters demonstrate. Always run your eyes over the back of the hand first, as it is a great lead-in before you tackle the palm on the other side.

Hair on the Back of the Hands

To be thorough in palmistry it is important to study the significance of any hair visible on the back of the hands or fingers. The hair can be regarded as an additional guideline. Originally it was believed that hair on the hands meant the person had a masculine, cruel streak. My experience is that it reveals far more than this.

Apart from body hair being a protection for the part of the body on which it appears, it is important to understand its origins. Just as the nail is the hoof of the human, growing out from the fingertips and imbued with the body's life force, so too does each hair come from this essence within.

Generally, the broader and coarser the hair, the greater the physical stamina. The finer the hair becomes, the less vital energy is present. Observe, too, whether the hair grows thickly or sparsely. The more hair is present, the stronger the physical constitution. With thick hair, there is usually a busy mind and a stable, self-possessed nature. Thinner hair suggests less physical robustness, and a disinclination to display emotion. Although they have a less active mind and fewer ideas, those that do emerge will be more refined.

Always pay attention to the skin texture beneath the hair, as this gives additional insights.

Thick and Fine Hair shows a person whose energy comes in short bursts.

Sparse Fine Hair suggests a weak personality.

No Hair Present indicates an extremely refined way of doing things, avoiding the physical.

Hair on the Thumb attests to a highly imaginative and inventive personality.

Hair on all the Fingers shows a predisposition to hard work and constant striving.

Thick and Coarse Hair indicates a down-to-earth nature.

Colour of Hand Hair

The colour of the hair on the hands and fingers can give us valuable information when combined with the insight provided by its placement and texture.

Black Hair shows a strong and true personality but can be a little broody. Inclined to secretiveness but very affectionate. Likes to argue.

Brown Hair shows a salt-of-the-earth temperament, but can be slow to take action. Generally placid and extremely reliable.

Blonde Hair on the positive side shows intelligence and a good mind full of bright ideas. On the downside, it can show a lack of confidence and one who is easily influenced.

Red Hair shows that one is excitable and too quick to rise to provocation. Tendency to be passionate sexually.

Grey Hair underlines life's transition time. It is reassessment time, with decisions to be made. In a younger person it indicates anxiety.

Silver Hair shows one who is unbiased by nature, with no need to dominate others.

White Hair shows that wisdom has arrived. The brain is used rather than brawn.

THREE

FINGERS AND
Their
Meanings

The length of each finger tells its own story. It gives a great deal of information regarding temperament and the way we express ourselves. When viewing a finger be aware of its shape and size, length and flexibility, and all of the aspects as given in this chapter. Always look at the fingers first on the top side of the hand, where the nails, finger joints and knuckles can be seen. Then turn the hand over to the palm side and view the underside of the finger to see the fingerprints and phalanges (Chapter 7). Many hands have a combination of fingers so you will need to refer to the basic quality relating to a specific finger, plus the basic formation of it. Each of the four fingers stands on its own and must be recognized as such.

The Names of the Fingers

Each of the fingers can be referred to by several names, depending on the palmist or the palmistry text. The following table gives the most commonly used names. In order to familiarize the new palmist with these names, references in the text to a particular finger may utilize any of the various names for that finger.

1st Finger	2nd Finger	3rd Finger	4th Finger
Index	Middle	Ring	Little
Jupiter	Saturn	Apollo	Mercury
		Sun	Liver, Health Line

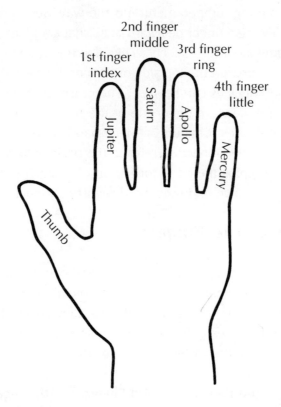

Figure 3: The Fingers

For the purposes of palmistry, the thumb is not considered a 'finger', and its properties are discussed in a following chapter.

The Length of the Finger

The Medium Finger

Fingers are average length when the middle finger, laid flat and bent down towards the wrist, comes to just over two thirds of the way down the palm. This length indicates a general overall balanced outlook towards life. The person will not run to extremes. A genial disposition.

The Long Finger

To check whether the fingers are long, bend them close to and flat against the palm. If any of the fingers reach nearly to the wrist then they can be considered long. The long-fingered are more competitive by nature. They are subtle in their approach and always think before they leap, patient if perhaps a little boring. Can be insipid and too retiring. A great eye for detail.

The Short Finger

The short middle finger, when bent down the palm towards the wrist, ends half-way down or less. The person with short fingers has a knack of seeing everything on a scale larger than life. Very quick with advancing new projects. Can be impulsive and inclined towards the slapdash. Rushes in where fools fear to tread. Unconventional thinker.

The Width of the Finger

Medium-Width Finger

The average-width finger will give an even balance to both the positive and the negative aspects of that particular finger. Overall its traits lean towards the positive, unless there is only one average-shaped finger on a hand, wherein the other traits will predominate.

Thin Finger

The thin finger indicates an active and intuitive nature. They will not linger on any project for too long. Extremely elegant and stylish. Gentle by nature, the peace makers of this world.

Fat Finger

The bigger or wider the finger becomes the more they indulge in the pleasure of life such as food, drink and sex. Can be overweight and clumsy. The tough business man. Down to earth.

Finger Texture

The Smooth Finger

People with smooth fingers are usually impulsive and have great physic ability if the finger is thin. Rather too quick in decision making before weighing up the facts, they tend to create a lot of unnecessary problems for themselves. Smooth-fingered people work from their intuition and hunches rather than from logic. This can cost them dearly sometimes. Extremely expressive emotionally.

The Rough, Bumpy Finger

This is known as the knotty or philosophical finger, where the knuckles and second finger joints protrude. This is not to be confused with arthritis. The skin is usually much coarser on this type of finger. Yields a very strong analytical mind that can always size up the situation. They can always see past any kind of deception, and have a good eye for business. Emotional expression is difficult, though. They do not like small talk, guard their privacy and are very thoughtful and weigh everything up. Hate gossip and look for the deep meanings for events rather than the glamour. Detached.

Flexibility of the Fingers (Bending Backwards)

Flexible Fingers

When the fingers can be bent backwards towards the back of the hand so that an arch is made of the hands then the person has an unusual outlook on life. Extremely unconventional. Can be far too generous. The supple-fingered have an ability to be adjustable. They are inclined not to take life too seriously as the belief is that everything will always turn out for the best. Fingers that naturally seem to flare backwards away from the palm show a love of life – they seek adventure wherever they can. Happy disposition.

Stiff Fingers

Fingers that appear rigid and do not seem to have any flexibility or looseness of joints at all, reveal an upstanding righteous nature. Do not like change and are stuck with a very formal code of behaviour. Very upright and stalwart, they find it difficult to enjoy themselves. They never loan money!

(Bending Forwards)

Flexible Fingers

Fingers are flexible when the thumb is capable of being pulled forwards towards the inside of the arm, to lay alongside the wrist. Decisions are difficult because of the flexible ability to see the other point of view. Rather inclined to be put-upon by others, who mistake their kindness for weakness. Extremely good at social gatherings. Always look on the bright side.

Stiff Fingers

When the fingers seem to bend forward only a fraction toward the palm, the person has a fear about something. It is as if they need to cover up. They do not like to be exposed.

Spaces

Spaces Between the Fingers

Look for two basic understandings when gauging the spaces between the fingers. Place the hand flat on a surface or hold the hand up in the air. Note if the fingers naturally stay close together or whether they cling to each other remaining closed and gap-free.

Average Open Fingers

They take everything in their stride. Do not like extremes. Promote harmony peace and goodwill. Live a balanced life.

Widely-Spread Fingers

When the hand is held upright in the air and the fingers fall naturally apart you can expect the person to go their own way. They do not like to be fenced in and need their own space. A love of adventure is indicated when the fingers are wide-spread leaving big spaces. Easy going, flower-power types.

Close-Together Fingers

When the fingers are held together with no gaps between them, they show a conventional personality. They like law and order and are not fond of the old making way for the new. A very private person, almost secretive. Can be mean of spirit and with money. Insecure. The Taxman!

Position

How the fingers are set into the palm can give valuable information at a glance. Always look at the palm side of the hand with the fingers fully stretched to get a proper view of the alignment at the base of the finger. If they all line up together in a straight line, there is an indication of success. Any finger set below another loses some of its power.

Perfect Finger Positioning – Straight Line

When the fingers appear to be set equally into the palm so that a straight line appears above the Mounts, it indicates a possibility of success in all areas. They usually do well in life.

Imperfect Finger Positioning – The Arch

When the fingers are set so that the line of their joining forms an arch starting from the index finger, the highest-set finger, and slopes down towards the Mercury finger, then the power of all the fingers will be diminished to a certain degree according to how low the fingers are set into the palm. Life will be a struggle.

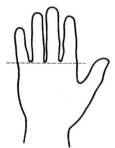

Arch – set fingers –
palm view

Straight – set fingers –
palm view

Figure 4: Finger Positions

Individual Finger Positioning

The Jupiter Finger

If the index finger is set lower than the others, opposite to its setting in the Arch, then the Jupiter qualities of that finger will be weakened. Less able to be the pioneer and forceful in work and play. Rather inclined towards a lot of talking but not much action.

The Saturn Finger

It is unusual to see a low-set middle finger, as it is the balancer of the hand. If, however, it is lower than the rest of the fingers the person will have problems coming to grips with life, particularly with family and relationships.

The Apollo Finger

When the third finger is set lower than the rest the person will spend their lives exerting their energies towards others at the expense of themselves. Inclined to give a lot out for no return. Personal happiness eludes them.

The Mercury Finger

The fourth finger set low into the palm indicates considerable struggle throughout life. Lack of influence in all areas. Circumstances are always against them.

Finger Tilting

When a finger leans towards another finger it takes on significant changes according to which finger it is leaning towards.

The Tilting Jupiter Finger

(A) Leaning Towards the Thumb
Inclined to quell any impulses. More interested in their homes than their businesses.

(B) Leaning Towards the Second Finger
The weight of responsibility is lighter. Hobbies play a prominent part in their lives.

The Tilting Apollo Finger

(A) Leaning Towards the Middle Finger
Environment as a child was against them. No parental or appropriate support was given.

(B) Leaning Towards the Little Finger
Pursues only monetary goals. Usually has a totally undisciplined attitude.

The Tilting Mercury Finger

(A) Leaning Towards the Third Finger
Inclined to use manipulation to get their needs met, but met they will be!

(B) Leaning Away from the Third Finger
Only interested in being self-employed. Must have personal freedom at all costs.

Fingers and Their Characteristics

Always consider the meaning of each finger by itself. Each finger is named from and takes the quality of the Mount (Chapter 17) under it. The index or first finger is known as Jupiter. The second or middle finger is Saturn. The third is called Apollo and the little or fourth finger is named Mercury. The thumb is not regarded as a 'finger' and is considered separately.

The Jupiter Finger

Brave Heart
The index finger, known as the finger of Jupiter, symbolizes zest, energy, drive, go-for-it: the finger of ambition. If this finger is longer than the others it shows a natural born leader and a talent for business, which leads to the personality being a little dominating and controlling. If the finger is shorter than the rest of the fingers then the person has had a bad start in life regarding development of their talents. Their desires did not figure much as far as the family was concerned. This manifests as a lack of confidence in adult life with a tendency to under value themselves.

The index finger points the way – it encourages the pioneer and is the leader in authority. It is the explorer, not afraid to experience and conquer new territory. An average-length Jupiter finger that is straight shows a person able to tackle whatever comes their way and has a naturally opportunistic attitude towards life and its adventures. Seizes the day always.

Length of Jupiter Finger

Long Jupiter Finger The pushy workaholic that lets nothing get in his way. Rather inclined to over-shadow people because he has to be the one giving the orders. Can get carried away with delusions of grandeur.

Short Jupiter Finger Very reticent and inclined to poor judgement. They are intimidated easily but they usually are considerate towards other people.

The Saturn Finger

Family Moralist

The middle finger is known as the finger of Saturn. It symbolizes family responsibility, study, caution and integrity. As it is the finger in the middle of the hand it balances both the heart and the head together. If there is a struggle between the head and the heart, the length of this finger will determine the outcome. Tries very hard to have a conventional family life. Respects law and order. Loves every-thing in its place. The Saturn influence brings about a steadiness, a conformity to all endeavours.

Average Length

When the Saturn finger is of average length, which is half a phalange longer than the index finger, the person veers toward the more positive aspects of its nature, resulting in a more contented and happier existence. Although life will still be taken seriously they will be able to lighten up a little so as to avoid 'all work and no play makes for a dull day'.

Long Length

The person with a long finger of Saturn is a worrier, consumed with grief and guilt over the seemly ordinary issues. They usually have a hard struggle in reaching their goals. Not the most light-hearted of companions, nonetheless they are hard workers and reliable and dependable. Being such deep thinkers, they can become gloomy from dwelling far too long on insurmountable problems. The introvert.

Short Length

The loner who tends to become melancholy. A heaviness in attitude combined with pessimism can unfortunately lead to depression. Because the middle finger holds the balance, one's aptitudes can go two ways. A short finger can show an easing up towards the responsibilities and concerns about life, freeing one to lead a more creative and happier existence.

The Apollo Finger

Personal Success

The third finger, known as the Apollo finger, deals with personal success, fulfilment and happiness. Dealing with all aspects of emotional expression, it is also known as the Sun Finger. With charm and geniality attributed to the Apollo character, they often can be seen working in the field of show business and the media. There is a flare and spontaneity that loves life and does not take kindly to being tied down to domesticity. They have a firm belief in their Apollo message, which is: 'are you willing to create the possibility of unlimited possibilities?' A lover of people and parties and all areas where there is activity and stimulation. Variety is the spice of life. Mundane routine bores them senseless. The extrovert.

Average Length

The Apollo finger is considered average when it is the same length as the Jupiter finger. It enables the person to have personal success beyond monetary gain. There is always an appreciation of art and beauty. Adaptability is a keynote.

Long Length

When the Apollo finger is the second longest of all the fingers it is extremely lucky and fortunate – usually getting what they set their hearts on. Winners in gambling. Can get carried away with the emotion of the moment and lose their heads. Loves the drama of life and has an uncanny knack for getting their just desserts. They always get full recognition and rewards for their efforts. Truly blessed with the gift of gold from the Sun: the Midas touch.

Short Length

The short finger of Apollo rather dampens down the opportunities that are on offer. The shortness causes restriction and frustration. Usually slow to realize their own potential. Always seem to be short-changed.

The Mercury Finger

Freedom Messenger

The little fourth finger is known as Mercury, who is the messenger of the gods. Freedom of movement, communicating, sociability and mental agility are all aspects connected to this finger. Mercury is able to influence people by its tongue because it is very eloquent. Because it moves freely at the edge of the hand there is an independence of spirit that is crucial for its functioning. There is an ability to sell ideas. Extremely versatile and flexible. Able to concentrate fully on one thing or many at the same time.

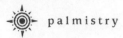

Average Length

The Mercury finger is of average length when the tip of the finger, when held flat against the Apollo finger, comes level with its first finger joint. The average-length Mercury finger gives a very positive advantage to the hand. No matter what may be happening elsewhere in the person's life they will always have the ability to speak up for themselves. They grasp the basic fundamental issues so are therefore not hindered or fooled.

Long Length

There is often an ability to be a writer as there is a great command of the written word. Excellent powers of self-expression which lead to the great orators. Good teachers and communicators. Full of ideas and versatile enough to span anything from the mysteries of the universe to commerce. Can become the guru or the con man if the finger is crooked.

Short Length

Life is not so easy for the person with a short finger of Mercury. Unable to express themselves they are inclined to become sarcastic and blunt to the point of being rude. Extremely impatient and unhappy, and somehow they always seem to get left behind.

Fingertip Shapes

It is crucial to examine the tips of the fingers to get an understanding of the general hand shape. Whatever the dimensions of the hands, the end of the finger determines how the person puts themselves out into the market place. The fingertips may all be the same shape or there could be a mixture of different types. Whatever they are, take into account the meaning of each one to get information regarding the persons persona and reasons for behaviour. For a drawing of the shapes, refer to Figure 2 in Chapter 2.

The Square Fingertip

Down to earth. No nonsense. The worker who holds the fort for everyone else. Dislikes emotional outbursts. Rational and constructive. Practical.

The Conic Fingertips

Loves beauty and anything artistic. Extremely instinctive. The great hostess and diplomat resides here. Sophisticated and well groomed. Balanced.

The Psychic Fingertip

The mystic arts expert. Needs to be protected from the harshness of the outside world. Sensitive par excellence. Spiritualist.

The Spatulate Fingertip

Gregarious. Full of energy and go. The extrovert. The pioneer always ready to try out something new. Low boredom threshold. Original.

FOUR

THE

Thumb

To save a man's life against his will is the same as killing him.

QUINTUS MORATIUS AOCCUS

The thumb ranks very highly in palmistry, mainly because it separates us from the animals. Monkeys have a thumb but it is not very flexible as it usually works in conjunction with the other fingers. The human thumb, however, is able to function independently from the rest of the fingers. This gives the thumb an assertion signifying independent action. The thumbs, symbolizing our inner moral fibre, have developed along with us through time, becoming more adept and stronger as man developed technologically. The thumb is the leader of the fingers. It monitors the person's willpower and logical abilities. Combining as it does the past, present and future it can be linked to the Karmic aspect of our living which governs the cause and effect, connecting us to all our previous understanding. In a psychological vein, the thumb can propel us into the right action that we need to take for ourselves. The thumb is the collective consciousness, the third eye for the hand. Hindu palmists consider the thumb so important that they read the thumb only. It is said that its circuit is the most sacred.

The thumb gives insights into our character. It strengthens our ego and our level of life-force energy in our daily workings with the outside world. The thumb represents power and shows by its size its strength and ability to express it. A hand that may appear weak can be immensely enhanced by a large thumb, just as a strong palm can be diminished because of a small thumb. The shape of the thumb, like the shape of the fingers, affects the attitude towards life.

Position of the Thumb

Medium-Set Thumb

When medium-set, the thumb emerges midway from between the bottom of the index finger and the wrist. All of the thumb's positive attributes will be easily accessed with this positioning.

High-Set Thumb

A thumb set higher up the palm nearer the bottom of the index finger shows a tendency to meanness and a lack of adaptability. Tends to withhold energy. Fears going with the flow.

Low-Set Thumb

The nearer the wrist the thumb is set, the keener the mind, plus an easier-going, generous nature. Adaptable, the independent who takes risks.

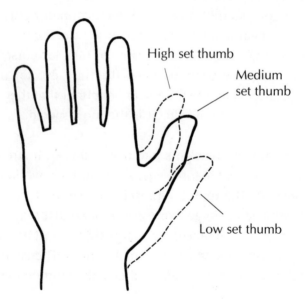

High set thumb

Medium set thumb

Low set thumb

 Figure 5: Positions of the Thumb

Flexibility of the Thumb

Close to the Palm
If the thumb seems to stay stuck to the side of the palm, then the person does not expose themselves. They are very careful with their money, and are very rigid morally.

Away from the Palm
A thumb that extends away from the palm when in repose shows a disposition to spend too much money. The further it extends, the more extravagant the person. Very easy, genial nature.

Length of the Thumb

Normal Length for the Thumb
A normal length is gauged when the thumb reaches as far as the lower phalange of the Jupiter finger. This allows all the best attributes to come to the fore, such as strength and the ability to press on regardless.

Long Thumb
When the tip of the thumb extends way beyond the lower part of the index finger, then the person is totally at ease with themselves. They are their own master. Could be too much into the head.

Short Thumb
A short thumb means a generally weak disposition. Difficulty is experienced in getting projects finished. Inclined to follow the crowd. No convictions.

The Two Sections of the Thumb

The thumb is divided up into two sections, and is best viewed from the reverse side for reading. The third section is the ball of the thumb, and is known as the Mount of Venus (Chapter 17). The first two sections of the thumb work in conjunction with each other. Ideally it is best to have both of them measuring the same.

The First Section of the Thumb

The Will Section

This is the top half of the thumb where the nail is. It represents the will and how good we are at getting our own way. When the top of the thumb bends over a little so that a curve appears it indicates that we like our own way and we are usually good at getting it. When it curves to the extreme it indicates the gambler. If the first section is stiff and upright, it shows that the person will be rigid in their opinions and extremely stubborn. They take a lot of convincing to change their opinions once their minds have been made up. An unyielding nature.

The Second Section of the Thumb

The Logic Section

This section shows our reasoning power and logic. It should be the same length as the first section of the thumb, which shows a balance between thought and action. If it is not then the person ruminates. They take such a long time making their minds up that unfortunately they miss the boat. This will be seen when it is much longer than the first section. When this section is shorter than the will-phalange then too much caution stifles any progress.

Additional material on the thumb's sections (phalanges) appears in Chapter 7.

Thumb Tip Shapes

To understand the thumb fully, it is important to recognize the shape of the tip of the thumb. These relate to the shapes of the hands and give an insight into the thumb's characteristics.

Conic-Tipped Thumb
A nice rounded tip to the thumb shows a great decisiveness and staying power. The most positive aspect of the top end of the thumb, is that if you *will* it so, you become the creator of possibility itself. The less rounded tip gives way to lack of resistance and the energy scatters.

Pointed or Psychic-Tipped Thumb
A thin, flat tip to the end of the thumb, can be seen when you hold the thumb side on. It reveals a highly-strung and nervous nature. Extremely sensitive. Kindness works wonders for the bearer this particular tip of the thumb.

Square-Tipped Thumb
The person who is fortunate enough to have this shaped thumb will have no worries about getting on in the world, because they have the ability to organize. Extreme stamina.

Spatulate Tipped-Thumb
Great flair for the owner of this shaped tip. A zest for living coupled with dynamism. Things happen around this person.

Deformed Tip of Thumb

When a bulbous, clubbed thumb tip appears it will seem very large and top-heavy. In palmistry it is considered to be a somewhat unwanted shape to have, as it is referred to as the murderous thumb. It must be borne in mind that it basically means the person withholds energy to such an extent that they have sudden outbursts of destructive temper. Unfortunately when this pent-up energy bursts its bank it can result in physical and psychological illness.

The Waisted Thumb

This thumb shows a definite narrowing as it gets nearer the knuckle, and flares out again the same as our waist does. It indicates that the person is very diplomatic in their approach to life. Great charm and logic if perhaps a little evasive.

FIVE

THE

Knuckles

The Knuckles are the four joints that protrude from the base of the fingers, on top of the hand where the fingers join. They come in basically two shapes: large and raised or flat and low. A large knuckle implies high intelligence whilst the flat knuckle is more creative. Also patience is implied for a high knuckle and impatience for a flat. Usually the knuckles come in three sizes: large, overlarge, and flat. The knuckles can vary tremendously from one hand to another.

Always observe the texture of the skin running over the knuckles. Smooth skin indicates impetuousness and rough, knotty skin indicates a cautiousness.

The Large Knuckle

When the knuckle protrudes and is raised up a little when the fingers are outstretched, it shows good intelligence that has been allowed to develop educationally. Generally a pleasant disposition as they have had a fair share of attention from parents and society. Ever-patient and shows a love of law and order.

The Overly Large Knuckle

Determined to do what they want. Extremely single-minded and self-orientated. The entrepreneur. Scientist.

The Flat Knuckle

Inclined to be more artistic in attitude. Finds it difficult to concentrate so energies get scattered. Impatient and forgetful.

Knuckles Differing Between Right and Left Hands

If they are flat on the *potential* hand and raised on the *hand of the future* then the person may have had a poor start academically in life but they have the possibility to be a mature student. Another understanding is that the person has learnt to engage their brain before they speak. When the knuckles are reversed and the potential hand has raised knuckles and the hand of the future has them low and flat, it means the person had the advantages when young but has not done anything with them.

The Finger Joints

It is important for the development of the finger's joints to be taken into account when reading the hand. There are two sets of finger joints on each of the four fingers. They are the junctions between the sections of the finger, called the phalanges, which are read from the palm side. These joints divide the finger up into three sections, and are inclined to stop the flow of energy of that particular finger when poorly developed. Thus it is important to understand their meaning, to see if they enhance or impede. They are either *flat*, which gives the hand a flat look when outstretched, or *knotted*, which protrude when the hand is outstretched. In the following lists of characteristics, any particular characteristic is given prominence according to the prominence of the joint; protruding joints more, flat joints less.

The First Set of Joints are below the finger-nail between the first and second phalanges, and deal with all matters regarding intelligence and the mind: the ability to organize themselves and their ideas, and orderliness. There is a loathing of muddles and untidiness.

The Second Set of Joints lies above the knuckle, between the second and third phalanges. This set is materially-oriented, with a love of possessions and a beautiful home. If a strong Head Line is present in the palm, a prominent joint indicates good business acumen. It will support those who look before they leap.

Characteristics for the Flat Finger Joint

When flat, the person is inclined to be impulsive and jump to conclusions. When working from a natural creative talent, they are less inclined to make mistakes. If the individual's work needs a lot of precise calculation, then smooth joints will be a hindrance.

There is also a love of grandeur, and the entrepreneur is highlighted here.

Characteristics for the Knotty Finger Joint

The protruding finger joint shows a meticulous temperament. They work well with details and can always see and pinpoint the real issue. Not impressed with get-rich-quick schemes. They need time to consider things before they act. The philosophers reside here.

THE NAILS
and Quick

It is a miracle when one realizes that when the electrical fluid flow that escapes from us through our fingertips solidifies it becomes a horn, which is called a nail. Our nails, the human hoof, are a visible print-out of the past internal happenings within ourselves. It takes the nails about six months to grow from the base to the end. The length to which a nail grows beyond the fingertip is of no consequence as far as the palmist is concerned. Only the nail still attached to the skin is looked at. In making an assessment through the nails, the base of the nail records recent happenings and where it stops growth and is still attached to the skin of the finger, gives information on that which happened at least 6 months ago. The middle of the nail thus registers the events of three months past.

Apart from being a half-year calendar they are extremely useful in diagnosing ailments and diseases. The old country doctor always took the nails into account whilst making an assessment of a patient's health following the tradition that the Romans set many centuries earlier. Today many a practitioner in the medical profession is well versed in the art of palmistry, including psychic observations of the nails, referring to it as Dermatoglyphic terminology.

The Shape of the Nails

The shape of the nails, which can be seen at a glance, can give valuable information about both the character and health of the individual. The shape indicates which diseases and ailments you may have a tendency towards.

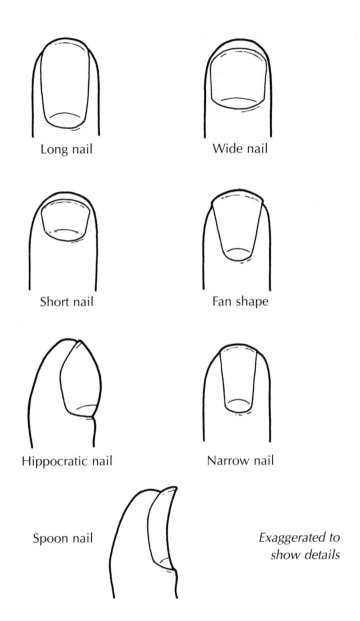

Long nail

Wide nail

Short nail

Fan shape

Hippocratic nail

Narrow nail

Spoon nail

Exaggerated to show details

Figure 6: Nail Shapes

The Average-Shape Nail

The average nail shape should appear not to be too long or short, wide or narrow according to the thickness of the finger it is on. It should fit in evenly. The ideal is to have a nail that is smooth and flexible without any fluting/ridges or marks on it, with a nice pink colour.

Character
Possessing these near perfect nails produces an even-tempered person. Not inclined to go to extremes.

Health
Generally well and robust. Able to recover from any physical problems. No major illness usually befalls them.

The Long Nail-Shape

The nail is considered long when it is twice the length of its width. It has the appearance of a long tube.

Character
Loves the finer things of life. Drawn to the arts and beauty. Excels in design as they are perfectionists.

Health
Vulnerable to all conditions relating to the immune system. A need to keep all bodily eliminations flowing freely, particularly the bowels.

The Wide Nail-Shape

This nail is very broad and seems to spread itself right across the finger.

Character
Broadminded, showing an expansion of views and ideas. Wholehearted with a manner that seems larger then life. Good manual workers.

Health
Inclined to ailments of the chest and throat area.

The Short Nail-Shape

The length of the short nail is equal to or less than its width.

Character
Critical by nature of oneself and others. Can be very impatient. Likes to argue. Touchy. Blunt.

Health
Prone to depression and headaches with a disposition to occasional heart problems.

The Fan-Shaped Nail

The fan-shaped nail can be recognized by its narrowness at the base of the nail and the broadness at the top. The appearance resembles a fan that is opened.

Character

A very active dynamic personality which runs on nervous energy. Easily frustrated.

Health

A disposition to chronic nervous disorders, breakdowns and psychosomatic illness.

The Hippocratic Nail-Shape

The Hippocratic nail can be identified by the way it bulges out from the finger, particularly when viewed from the side. It is also known as the 'watch hour-glass' nail because it resembles a clock face.

Character

Extremely bright and bubbly by nature. Likes to study and achieve.

Health

A person with this shape nail is advised not to smoke at any account. Even avoid sitting in a room with others smoking because the lungs will not tolerate it. Inclined to be overweight and to have allergies.

The Narrow Nail-Shape

The narrower a nail becomes the weaker the ability to get things done, regardless of whether the nail is short or long.

Character

A narrow-nailed person does not like to be rushed. They take one thing at a time. Life is lived at a slower pace.

Health

Not robust by nature but able to live an active life provided they do not neglect themselves.

The Spoon Nail-Shape

This nail appears to dent inwards, almost as if a scoop has been taken out of it. This can easily be seen from the side view with its concave shape.

Character

Extremely sensitive emotionally. Rather inclined to bottle things up.

Health

Needs plenty of rest. Nutritionally deficient. Inclined to chronic skin problems. Prone to underactive thyroid.

The Four Basic Nail Qualities

There are four basic nail qualities. First establish the shape of the nail from the previous section. Now see if that shape has a quality-shape that goes along with it. For instance you could have a long-shaped nail that is basically round or square, conic or spatulate. Just add the meaning of the Basic Nail Quality to the Shape meaning to get a fuller picture.

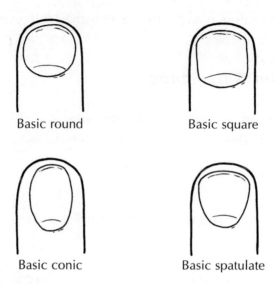

Basic round   Basic square

Basic conic   Basic spatulate

Figure 7: Four Basic Nail Qualities

Basic Round Nail

A round quality to the nail adds an easy-going nature. Genial and good humoured.

Basic Square Nail

Down to earth. No nonsense or frills. Very dependable. A stickler for details.

Basic Conic Nail

Almond in shape, these nails move towards sophistication. Lives in harmony and beauty. Adaptable. Seeks fun and enjoyment.

Basic Spatulate Nail

Extremely excitable. Loves new adventures, interesting projects and conversations.

Texture of the Nails – The Health Factor

The texture of the nails can give indications regarding the health of the owner. This should always be checked with a doctor.

Hard Nails
The person may have deficiency in the glandular system such as an under-active thyroid or pituitary gland.

Soft Nails
There is a possibility of a protein deficiency. Disposition to arthritis.

Flaky Nails
Look for nutrition deficiencies, a lack of calcium, extreme lethargy.

Nail Markings

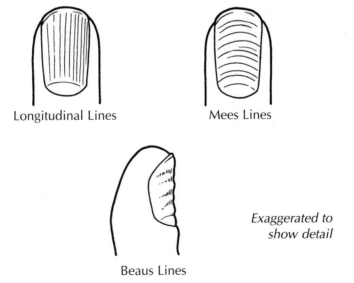

Longitudinal Lines   Mees Lines

Beaus Lines

Exaggerated to show detail

Figure 8: Nail Markings

The nails can have distinct markings on them caused by life events and health issues.

Longitudinal Ridges

Longitudinal lines are ridges that appear to be running from the top of the nail straight down to the base vertically. These lines or ridges indicate that rheumatism is possible at some time in the person's life. There is a possibility of colitis or hyperthyroidism.

Mees Lines

These show up on the nails as lines running horizontally across the nail, and are relatively flat seen edge-on. It can show that the person may have experienced a high fever in the last six months. Can indicate an inclination to coronary heart disease. May show a poisoning of the system, especially arsenic.

Beaus Lines

The beaus lines manifest as gouges horizontally across the nail. As opposed to the Mees Lines, the nail looks wavy, dipping up and down. Each dip may indicate that the person has received a shock at that time or experienced emotional trauma. Acute infections and poor diet are another possible cause.

The Colour of the Nails

The colour that shows through from underneath the nail gives interesting clues regarding health conditions.

Pink Nails

Pink nails are the most desired colour to have as this confirms a healthy body.

White Nails

A slow metabolism which gives limited energy. Could indicate anaemia deficiency, or other blood conditions

Yellow Nails

Bile in the blood – jaundice present. Disturbances in the digestive system. Liverish.

Blue Nails

Heart conditions. The term 'blue baby' came from children born with heart irregularities who showed a blue tinge to the nails. Poor circulation.

Dark Red Nails

When the top of the nail appears very dark whilst the rest of the nail is red this shows hypertension. Extreme stress and pressure is present in the person's life.

The Colour of Spots on the Nails

Any spots or pits that appear on the nails can be assessed by their colour.

Flesh-Coloured Spots

When little flesh-coloured pits appear on the nails it shows there has been a general debilitation health-wise. The person will be run down. Minor ailments such as flu or colds can cause pits or spots to be formed.

White-Coloured Spots

Can indicate a calcium deficiency but it usually indicates exhaustion and excessive fatigue.

Black-Coloured Spots

Do not confuse black-coloured spots on the nail with the colour that comes from bruising. A black spot on the nail can show problems with the heart. Psychologically a black spot can reveal that the person's life was on hold at that particular time.

During a reading you should always bear in mind that any suspicions of medical irregularities should be referred to a doctor, and not 'diagnosed' by the reader.

The Quick or Cuticle

The quick on a nail has its place in palmistry although it is often left out – provided the nails have not been manicured, where it is usually removed. The placement of the quick or cuticle on the nail and how far it grows up gives us information regarding the ability of the character to follow through with the traits that are attached to the finger that it is on. The quick is the protector of the nail. It is a membrane that seals the exit of the nail from the soft fleshy base from which it has emerged.

Medium Quick

A medium quick which grows onto the nail from the edge of the skin, should just stretch over so that it forms a nice firm ridge running around the nail. It will seal the young nail growing from the finger bed. The temperament will be even and there will be a good balance between expansion and contraction. In other words, knowing when to go and when to stop.

Long Quick

This is where the quick grows a long way up the nail. It sometimes seems to almost cover the nail. This person will show a need for security. They are secretive and will have difficulty in getting their needs met as others will not know what they want. They have experienced loss of trust somewhere in their lives.

Absent Quick

When there is no quick connecting onto the nails the person is rather vulnerable, and inclined to leave themselves exposed. They appear to be a pushover and lacking in self-esteem.

Split Quick

Quicks can be torn, rugged and split. This shows the person is worried and has a lot of opposition facing them. Low physically.

Hanged-Nail Quick

Here the outside of the nail seems to join the edge of the quick and pulls away from the finger. It can become extremely painful and sore. It is important when it is like this not to get it infected – it should be cut down immediately so that it doesn't tear too deeply. Shows the person is under pressure and is trapped in a situation that doesn't suit them so the quick and nail literally break away, which is what they would like to do.

Moons

The moons on a nail give an indication of the person's physical constitution. They appear as a half-circle coming up from the base of the nail, ideally in a shade of pale pink. The question is whether moons are present or not. It is desirable to have a medium-sized moon on each nail.

WAY of

Medium-Sized Moon

When there is a medium-sized moon on each finger the person will have a splendid constitution, robust and full of energy.

Large-Sized Moon

A large cuticle which appears to cover half the nail indicates hyperactivity from a banking up of excess energy that cannot escape. A tendency towards high blood pressure.

Absence of Moons

If there are no moons on the fingernails the constitution will be delicate. But there is no need for despair as the flesh may be weak but the spirit can be strong. Moons can also disappear when they have been present: this foretells that ill health could be on its way. The moon can reappear again when health returns.

Thumb-Only Moon

When the moon appears only on the thumb it is a good sign as it strengthens everything all-round – both the physical body and the mental abilities.

SEVEN

FINGERPRINTS
and
Phalanges

Fingerprints (Dermatoglyphics)

Each person's skin pattern is totally unique, which is why finger-printing by the police is crucial for identifying criminals. In China, the Emperor's thumb-print was often used instead of a signature on state documents. Dermatoglyphics is also used in the fields of genetics and medicine. It is a sure way of confirming Downs Syndrome, known as mongolism, by the abnormal fingerprint pattern taken at birth. Medical research is currently underway with the new-born in an attempt to discover whether certain fingerprint patterns give an indication of future ailments or diseases. The fingerprints are well established on the foetus about eighteen weeks after conception. Unlike other marks on the hand, once set they never change. Even if the skin is burnt off, they grow back in exactly the same pattern of ridges as before.

The formation of the lines acts a channel for sweat, a stimulator for nerve endings, and as an aid in gripping. There are three ridge-patterns: loops, whorls, and arches. These patterns are not just confined to the fingertips. They can be found anywhere on the hands, particularly on the mounts. The patterns, wherever they are, give a guide to the personality.

Loop
Mild tempered. Straightforward. Quite lively. A very versatile mind.

Whorl
An individual with a strong definite personality. Potentially brilliant. Best self-employed.

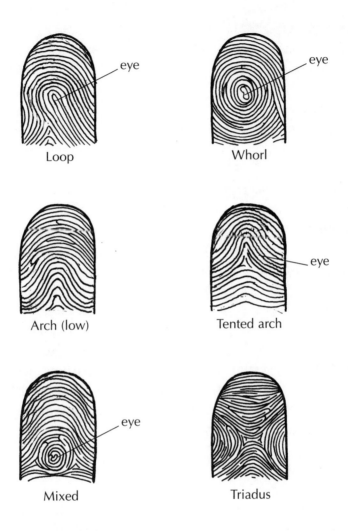

Figure 9: Basic Fingerprint Patterns

Arch (Low)

Can be hard-hearted and insensitive. Sceptical. Unemotional and materialistic.

Tented Arch

A highly-strung individual. Artistic. Impulsive but stubborn.

Mixed

The person is likely to be muddle-headed.

Triadus

This finger ridge pattern can be seen anywhere in the palm. Takes on aspects of its surroundings. Generally good fortune. Excitable.

Apex

In some fingerprint patterns there is a centre that looks like an eye (see Figure 9). Note where it appears on the finger. If it appears on the fingernail section of the finger, the person aims high in life. If on the middle segment of the finger, it shows a balance in all areas of life. If on the basal section, the person will have a down-to-earth approach to life.

The Phalanges

The fingers on the reverse side of the hand to the nails are divided up into three sections and are known as the phalanges. They are the fleshy lengths between the finger joints. The fingertip end is the first phalange, which governs the mental attitude. The middle segment is the second phalange, indicating emotional order. The base segment is the third phalange, which reveals our materialistic outlook on life. Each phalange on every finger has its own particular meaning. Account must be taken of which is the longest or shortest.

Ideally they should be all the same length, giving a balance in all areas. The longer a phalange is the more dominant that particular section of the finger becomes. The shorter it is the less efficient that part becomes.

Also check to see if the phalanges protrude from the finger like an elevated pad. The larger it is the more abundant the qualities will be, particularly if the third phalange of material gain is the most rotund. When the phalanges are flat and close to the finger-bone there will be a diminishing of their specific aspects. In coming to a conclusion about a phalange's vices or virtues always take into account the shape of the fingertips as well.

The Jupiter (Index) Finger Phalanges

First Phalange – Mental Attitude

Medium Length
Good respect for leadership. Self-esteem. Dominating. Very controlling.

Long Length
Overly-strong ego. Extremely decisive. Efficient. Independent thinker.

Short Length
Vain. Lack of self-confidence. Money orientated. Ignores opportunity.

Large and Bulbous
The bully. Hard taskmaster. Over-indulgent and given to excess.

Flat and Thin
Lack of expansion. Mean in body and spirit. Self-denial.

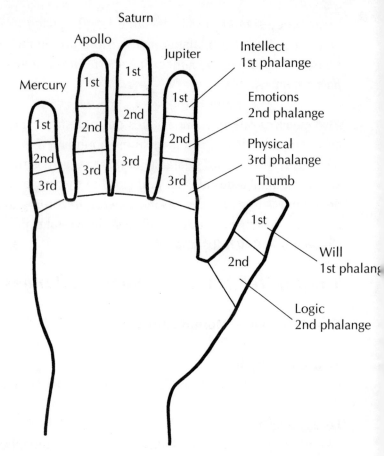

Figure 10: The Phalanges

Second Phalange – Emotional Order

Medium Length
Supports ambition. Love of heritage. Noble. Social climber.

Long Length
The entrepreneur. Gifted in business. Seeks relationships. Workaholic.
Loves tradition.

Short Length

Non-starter. Inhibited. Suspicious. Resentful. Unloved.

Large and Bulbous

Pompous. The name dropper. In love with their own publicity. Marries for position.

Flat and Thin

Lacks roots. Old fashioned. False pride. Extremely earnest Emotionally cold.

Third Phalange – Materialistic Outlook

Medium Length

Good balance between work and play. Rebuilder of ideals. The achiever.

Long Length

Idealist. Seeker of the creature comforts. Flamboyant. Generous.

Short Length

Short-changed. Lacks common sense. Loss of hope.

Large and Bulbous

Flaunts powers. Impractical ideas. Abuse of power. Over sexed. Greedy.

Flat and Thin

Brainwashed.

The Saturn (Middle) Finger Phalanges

First Phalange – The Fingertip Section

Medium Length
Studious. Good sense of responsibility. Solid and secure. Orderly.

Long Length
The egghead. Family tyrant. Reliable. Staid.

Short Length
Melancholy. Seeks solitude. Fly-by-night. The waster. The worrier.

Large and Bulbous
The fanatic. The guru. The righteous. Intellectual snob. A transformer.

Flat and Thin
Paranoid. Suspicious. Out of step. Hermit.

Second Phalange – The Middle Section

Medium Length
Down to earth. Loves the land. Productive. Progressive. The reformer.

Long Length
Committed to planetary improvements. Charitable. Believes in family life.

Short Length
Defensive. Late developer. Immature emotionally. Dislikes commitment.

Large and Bulbous
Staid. Stuck. Avoids change. Dogmatic. Chauvinist.

Flat and Thin
Frustrated. Careless. Resentful. Rejects emotional displays.

Third Phalange – The Basal Section

Medium Length
Rules hearth, home, and family. Socially conscious. Loves committee meetings.

Long Length
Avarice. Gains material wealth regardless. Hospitable. Serious.

Short Length
The drudge. Does things at the expenses of the self. Self pity. Gloomy.

Large and Bulbous
Spontaneous. Generous. Gambler. Practical idealist.

Flat and Thin
Miser. Denies the joys of the flesh. Fear of success. Loner.

The Apollo (Third/Ring) Finger Phalanges

First Phalange – The Fingertip Section

Medium Length
Optimistic. Versatile. The achiever without too much struggle. Common sense.

Long Length

Great improviser. The liberator. Artistically inspired. Winner all the way.

Short Length

Thwarted talents. Lack of personal happiness.

Large and Bulbous

Over estimate their own abilities and situations. Sloth. Immorality. Arrogant to the point of the ridiculous. The entrepreneur.

Flat and Thin

Fickle. The liquidator. Insane authoritarianism.

Second Phalange – The Middle Section

Medium Length

Personal success. Fulfilment and happiness.

Long Length

Social climber. Determined to be successful. Entertaining.

Short Length

Completely without rhythm. Lacks inspiration and lucky breaks.

Large and Bulbous

The fortune seeker. Prostitutes the self for sex and money.

Flat and Thin

Unmet opportunities. Unlucky love life. Low key lifestyle.

Third Phalange – The Basal Section

Medium Length
Abundance. Life's knocks seem to have passed one by. Contented with one's lot.

Long Length
Never has enough. Constantly striving for material gain. Discontented, always seeking.

Short Length
Inclined to give too much work for too little return.

Large and Bulbous
The show off. Larger than life personality. Invasive.

Flat and Thin
Always out of pocket. Into self-denial. Always seems to be in the wrong job, and at the wrong place and time.

The Mercury (Little) Finger Phalanges

First Phalange – The Fingertip Section

Medium Length
Always able to get their needs met. Lively mind. Great conversationalist.

Long Length
Eloquent – gifted with a silver tongue. Great reasoning and logical powers.

Short Length
Verbally inadequate. Mentally slow.

Large and Bulbous
Bombastic. Sunny disposition. Expansive. The big spender.

Flat and Thin
Agile. Quick thinker. Good salesman.

Second Phalange – The Middle Section

Medium Length
The arbiter. Diplomatic. Charmer for the opposite sex.

Long Length
The empire builder. Precise. Continually striving for fresh angles.

Short Length
Does not suffer fools gladly. Commercially astute.

Large and Bulbous
Over indulgent to staff and friends. Great solver of problems.

Flat and Thin
Slick and quick. Fast pace.

Third Phalange – The Basal Section

Medium Length
A craftsman with words and business deals. Good provider.

Long Length
The comedian. A lover of life. Pursues success in the media.

Short Length
The blunderer. Clumsy. Low business acumen.

Large and Bulbous
Dishonest. The con man. Continually talking. Believes own publicity.

Flat and Thin
Afraid of their own voice. Subdued.

Thumb

The thumb has two phalanges. The first one is connected to the will and the second is connected to logic. Ideally they are the same length as this gives a balanced outlook between the two.

First Phalange – The Fingertip Section

The top section of the thumb is known as the 'will' phalange. It gives an indicator of our will power.

Long Length
The longer it is the more determined the person is to get what they want – determination to the point of ruthlessness.

Short Length
Unable to get their own way. Needs go unmet as they are constantly overlooked.

Large and Bulbous
Great strength and stamina. They can push through regardless of what is put in their way.

Slender and Thin
Physically delicate. Extremely intuitive. Psychic. Great charmers.

Second Phalange – Middle Section

This second section deals with logic. It highlights our ability to work out what is the best action for us.

Long Length
The longer this section is the more the person procrastinates, thus reducing their chances of success. By the time they make their minds up it's too late.

Short Length
Rather inclined to leap before they think.

Large and Bulbous
Speaks their mind to the point of bluntness. Can be rude.

Slender and Thin
Avoid decision making. Proffer others to make their mind up. The follower.

Third Phalange

This is the ball of the thumb, which is the basal portion of the thumb extending into the palm. It is known as the Mount of Venus, and is covered in the chapter on The Mounts.

Thumb Phalanges of Unequal Length

The First Phalange Long and the Second Phalange Short
Rushes in without thinking first.

The First Phalange Short and the Second Phalange Long
Inclined to be thinkers and not doers.

Rings

The Significance of the Wearing of the Rings
Rings have been worn on the fingers almost as long as there have been people. It is a custom that goes back to the beginning of civilization and should not be regarded as a frivolous whim. Rings were originally worn as a symbol of power if worn by men, whether it was religious, military or political. The wearing of rings by women was connected to economics. It showed the value of her husband's or master's material wealth. The unmarried woman was often not allowed to wear rings.

Note which finger the ring is placed on as it gives emphasis to that particular finger. The colour of the ring and the stones also gives immense insight. The colour can reveal not only the reason for its being worn, but also the colour needed to heal any negative aspects both mentally and physically. For much as it highlights the positive qualities, its placing also provides information about negative traits.

In the section below on ring wearing, and their colour, both positive and negative reasons for the wearing of that ring are given. Embrace the positive aspects and seek to turn around any negative traits indicated.

Fashion can have an influence on how many rings are worn but it can be beneficial to spare a thought as to why or who dictates the trend. It will surely give a lot of information about *them*.

Ring Worn on Index Finger

Jupiter – a sign of power A ring worn on this finger shows a person's desire to dominate. History always depicts the famous and ambitious sporting a ring on this finger, as can often be seen on old paintings. While it is positive to have ambition, care must be taken not to crush others in its pursuit. *Often seen on a square hand.*

Ring Worn on Middle Finger

Saturn – a sign of balance Although a ring worn on this finger suggests a serious minded person it also reveals a person who tries to hide their insecurities behind a show of confidence. There is an inclination to be pessimistic. *Often seen on the psychic hand.*

Ring Worn on Third Finger

Apollo – a sign of sensitivity All matters emotional are connected to the third finger on either hand. The left hand's third finger is considered the closest to the heart. A ring worn here signals emotional attachment or the lack of it. The wearer should seek a fulfilling relationship, and let go of destructive ones. *Seen on all hand shapes.*

Ring Worn on Fourth Finger

Mercury – a sign of the rebellious A ring worn on the small finger indicates someone who prizes freedom above all else. When worn on the hand of potential a ring reveals that when they were children they needed special direction. On the hand of the future it shows someone who places their trust in money first, before emotions. The wearer must take care that the desired freedom does not become freedom at any cost. Learn to enjoy the fruits of one's labour. *Seen on all hand shapes.*

Ring Worn on the Thumb
The soul finger – the sign of strength The eccentric and ego power-trips are associated with the wearing of rings on this digit. The realities of life are distorted, and they only listen to their own needs. Remember that wealth is a matter of perspective – count your blessings. The exotic orchid grows not at the top of the mountain, but at the bottom in all the grime and darkness. *Seen on all hand shapes.*

Colour of Rings
The colour of the rings and their stones gives information about the wearer. Couple the colour understanding with the name of the finger and its meanings.

DIAMOND – WHITE

Positive Character	Endurance. Originality. Resurrection. Vision. Purity.
Negative Character	Misleading. Unreliable. Isolated. Soiled.
Physical Aspect	Lymphatic system

RUBIES – RED

Positive Character	Fighter. Dynamic. Courageous. Pioneer.
Negative Character	Guilt. Stubborn. The bully. Intolerant.
Physical Aspect	Sexual Organs. Circulation. Blood.

GARNET – BLACK RED

Positive Character	Strong. Willpower. Mature advisor. Stable.
Negative Character	Lecherous. Cruel. Stagnant. Molester.
Physical Aspect	Congealed blood. Clotting.

CITRON – YELLOW
Positive Character   Elimination. Confident. Just. Intellectual.
Negative Character   Limited. Sarcastic. Rigid. Ignorant.
Physical Aspect   Nervous system. Skin. Digestion.

SAPPHIRE – BLUE
Positive Character   Spiritual atonement. Integrity. Truthful.
Negative Character   Snobbish. Spiteful. Superstitious. Deceitful.
Physical Aspect   Over-active thyroid gland. Vocal cords. Upper lungs.

EMERALD – GREEN
Positive Character   Charitable. Tolerant. Abundant. Harmonious.
Negative Character   Jealous. Frustrated. Greedy. Unimaginative.
Physical Aspect   Thymus gland. Heart area.

TURQUOISE – GREEN/BLUE/YELLOW
Positive Character   Self-sufficient. Single minded. Ambitious. Calm.
Negative Character   Off hand. Deceptive. Resistant. Indecisive.
Physical Aspect   Healing colour for the central nervous system. Throat and chest.

GOLD – ORANGE/YELLOW
Positive Character   Sociable. Free. Triumphant. Future happiness.
Negative Character   Over indulgent. Fearful. Paranoid. Overbearing.
Physical Aspect   The gut. Lower intestines. Kidneys.

SILVER – WHITE

Positive Character	Illuminates. Fluid. Reflective. Unbiased.
Negative Character	Split. Elusive. Emotional restrictions. Wallowing.
Physical Aspect	Brings body and mind to maturity.

PLATINUM – GREY

Positive Character	Sane. Linking of Opposites. Realistic.
Negative Character	Caged. Impoverished. Melancholy. Austere.
Physical Aspect	Reveals imminent breakdowns. Strengthens.

AMETHYST – PURPLE

Positive Character	Self-employed. Dignified. The protector. Inventive.
Negative Character	Delusions of grandeur. Ruthless. Fraudulent. Corrupt.
Physical Aspect	Pineal gland. The brain. Scalp.

EIGHT

THE
Palms

Initially hand readings were done on only the back of the hand, using its shape, the shapes of the fingers, nails, etc. This gave the persona of the person, the outward picture they project to the public. It was only some centuries later that the then-modern palmist incorporated the palm on the inside of the hand with its lines, markings and mounts, revealing the person's true nature and inner heart's desires. That revealed by the palm can be completely opposite to the personality that is projected. The palm is the major area for giving hand analysis. In a sense palm reading can be compared to reading someone's private letters. The thickness and constancy of the palm along with the skin texture gives clues to our basic talents in life.

The Width and Thickness of the Palm

The way to test the thickness is to put your thumb in the middle of the palm, and the index finger on the top of the hand on the other side, and press them together to get an overall feeling of its thickness. You will also use this test for the Plain of Mars, in Chapter 18.

Normal Palms
The most desired palm should be in proportion to the thumb and fingers. When there is this balance, then whatever the rest of the hand reveals, it shows there is the intelligence and energy to overcome any obstacles. An ideal palm is firm without being too hard or too soft.

Over-Large Palm
If the palm is over-large for the rest of the hand – seen when the fingers appear extremely small relative to the rest of the palm – then too much force is put into activities. The trying-too-hard syndrome.

Under-Size Palm

When the palm appears to be too small there will be a lack of opportunities or the ones that present themselves will not be taken up.

Flabby Palm

A flabby, soft palm is inclined to be lazy and indolent, will always take the easy option. Over indulgent.

Thick Palm

When the palm is thick and firm there will be a no- nonsense nature which frequently causes quarrels. Great physical stamina.

Thin Palm

Usually lightweight in their approach to life. Good fun at a dinner party with an intelligent, witty repartee. The thinner it is the less physical strength there is, but what they lack physically they certainly make up intellectually. Good as a researcher and counsellor because of their mental alertness.

Hollow Palm

The hollow palm is where the centre of the palm has an indentation looking like a hollow, usually meaning a delicate physical constitution. Inclined to disappointment. Low energy threshold unless on the psychic hand shape, where it appears narrower than usual. Refined by nature; can be artistic. Needs to make sure that they don't do too much at the expense of themselves.

Skin Texture of the Palm

The finer the skin the greater chance the person has of remaining youthful. They will age extremely well.

Smooth Texture on a Hard Palm

The skin can be smooth on a hard hand. This indicates added depths of sensitivity to moderate any hardness in the nature. The coarser the skin becomes the less sensitive the nature, and the more down to earth one is.

Course Texture Skin on a Soft Palm

Toughens any softness in the personality.

Course Texture with a Hard Palm

Tough skin and a hard hand can take care of itself very well. A bit brusque at times.

Colour of the Palm

Almost every palm has a distinct colour. There are many nerves in the hand, particularly in the palm. Its colour is a good indicator of what is happening internally both mentally and physically.

Rise-Pink Palm

The most desired colour to have for a palm. Denotes an even temperament with a balance between rest and play.

Pale Palm

Needs to exercise to boost the immune system.

White Tinge to Palm

When the palm is a pale-white colour, it shows a fairly unemotional personality. The person often doesn't have much fun because they are caught up in petty worries.

Red Tinge to Palm

A red palm reveals pent-up energy. Can be quick of temper but has a lively nature. Excitable. Brilliant health, but tendency to high blood pressure.

Dark Red Tinge to Palm

Over indulges. Prone to excess. Can be the bully boy. Crude sensuality. Sluggish circulation.

Yellow Tinge to Palm

Chiefly indicates digestive disorders. Points to loss of faith in trust. Unhappy and suspicious. Nervous tendencies.

Blue Tinge to Palm

Cool disposition, reserved and aloof. The studious type. Always think before they leap. Health-wise watch heart, chest complaints.

Elemental Classification of Palm Shapes

Another way of reading the palms is by a more ancient system called Elemental Classification. It divides the hands into four types incorporating the elements of *Earth*, *Fire*, *Air* and *Water*. It is worth having a basic understanding of these four types which gives another approach to resolving questions and coming to conclusions whilst reading. You can add this type of *elemental* understanding and characteristics to the *classic* palm interpretation.

Earth Hand

The Earth hand appears much like the square hand. It is short, squarish and very strong, with fingers to match. The major lines on the palm appear deep and unbroken and it has a lack of finer lines. It is thought of as a practical hand. Possessors of the Earth hand may appear a little dull as companions but they are loyal and dependable. They have a desire to dominate, but are courageous and adventurous, the pioneers.

This hand is associated with masculine traits.

Air Hand

The Air type has a square palm and very long fingers, as opposed to the short fingers of the Earth hand. The major lines are usually strongly etched in the palm and even the minor lines will be well presented. Air types often have their heads up in the clouds and are the great thinkers and problem solvers, always mentally orientated. Quick witted, they are great communicators who think with the head rather than the heart.

This hand is associated with feminine traits.

Fire Hand

The Fire hand has short fingers and a long, oblong-shaped palm. Usually expressive by nature, they have intuitive tendencies. The possessors of the Fire hand are extroverts and inclined to changeable moods, with a tendency toward leaping before they have thought things through. The lines on the hand can be many but they will not be as prominent as the Earth and Air hand. Very emotional and can also be aggressive if pushed. Very affectionate and love to entertain their friends generously. Desire attention and must be the boss.

This hand is associated with masculine traits.

Water Hand

The Water hand is slim and long in both the palm and the fingers. It is usually a slender, delicate hand, similar to the psychic hand in shape. The lines are also fragile. The nature is very changeable, just the same as the sea or a river. It can reveal a shallow nature at one moment or there can be deep reservoirs of emotion the next. Very sentimental and receptive. Needs lots of support and encouragement. Must be careful not to pick up other people's problems, as they can tune in and absorb other's energies easily. They will do anything to avoid a fight. Soulful disposition.

This hand is associated with feminine traits.

NINE

THE LINE SECTION
and Life
Line

*Lines have not been traced without cause in the
hands of men; they evidently emanate from heaven
and from human individuality.*

ARISTOTLE

Introduction to the Lines

The lines on the palm are the part of palmistry that most people are drawn to first of all. They are a road map that can be compared to the motorways, highways and country lanes of life, indicating the major talents and energies we have at our disposal. They carry an electrical current which is influenced by an invisible fluid flow that goes backwards and forwards from the brain like the movement of traffic in and out of the heart of the city. Because of this fluctuation of the vital energies these lines are alive just the same as you are. These lines are not fixed and can change, just the same as you do when affected by life's experiences. It has been established that a person whose hand has become paralyzed will lose the lines on that hand. They disappear because the nerves are dead. The current has been switched off, whilst the active, alive hand will keep its lines as long as it is receiving the electrical flow.

Whilst these lines are crucial in giving information of past, present and future events, always remember to refer them to the shape of the individual's hand. A strong Head Line on a psychic hand shape will have to work harder to get their ideas into production as there will not be any grounded support from the intuitiveness of such a hand shape. Whereas a strong Head Line with a square-shaped hand will be backed up by this hand.

It is worth repeating that the lines have the ability to change. Nothing is fixed. If you see a break which causes disruption, or any other seemingly adverse marking which looks likely to be coming in the future, take heart, as pre-warning about events and happenings up front gives an immense advantage. It means you can always do something to turn it around.

The lines should be scrutinized carefully as many important finer lines and markings cannot be seen with the naked eye. A magnifying glass and bright light is essential if you are serious about getting a full picture regarding the information laid out before you.

The clearest lines are the most ideal. Life will be more straightforward and less trouble. Besides being readily visible the lines should have a reasonable depth to them. This adds strength to the line and its meaning. The weaker they are the less impact that particular line will have.

Compare the lines on both hands. If the hand of potential, which represents your *past*, shows a difficult Life Line, for example, whilst on the other hand, the active hand of today and the future, shows a stronger, clearer Life Line, then you know the person has overcome a lot of obstacles and resistance from their early life. It is likely that they have had to change their total outlook and direction. If, however, the person had a relatively good start in life and the active hand of now shows in its Life Line disappointments, recorded in the line by its markings, that is the point when the actual disruption occurred. It will show what happened in the person's life circumstances, and the influences that led the person astray from what appeared to be a promising start.

WAY of

For Line Reading

I will describe in depth the three major lines that everyone needs to understand first to get an immediate impression of where the person is coming from. It starts with the supreme line of all, the Life Line, followed by the Head Line and then the line of the Heart. The latter work alongside each other, as it is of no use to be all head and no heart – or the reverse. These two will show how the Life Line's potential will be carried out. We will then look to the fourth line which is the Fate Line, giving information about ambition and pioneering spirit. The fifth line, line of the Sun, shows family duties and career prospects. It also concerns itself with creativity and potential for personal success, fulfilment and happiness. The sixth line of Mercury, the Line of the Liver, also reveals health and social attributes.

These are the six major lines. Following the Major Lines section are the Minor Lines, which also have their individual meanings and which can influence and send energy to the major lines. The Timing of Events section and the sections on markings will clarify and pinpoint the happenings observed on the lines.

The lines appear on the inside of the palm, which is the area that reveals the true self. They are of major importance for enlightening and confirming events. In this and the following chapters, the positioning of the lines is sometimes described in relation to the Mounts. See Chapter 17 for the position of the Mounts.

The Life Line

The Governor General

> *The life which is unexamined is not worth living.*
>
> PLATO

The most important line on the hand is the Life Line. This master line has absolute supremacy over all other lines. It not only foretells longevity but also gives you immeasurable information on just about every other aspect of your life. If you can only study one line in Palmistry then this is it! Get the rudiments of this one and you will have the basic core of palmistry. Whatever line you read up on afterwards you will always have to refer back to the line of Life to come to a proper conclusion.

The Life Line does not just indicate how long you will live. Forget the old wives' tale that a short Life Line means a short life, as other factors in the hand can easily counteract that situation. What the Life Line does is give strength to the person's life energy force, and vitality. The longer and stronger the Line the greater the zest, energy and drive of the individual. No two Life Lines are the same, although most will conform to some basic patterning. In addition to physical vitality certain psychological traits can be seen. The Line reflects a person's heredity, so any breaks in the Line may show a change from tradition or from the lifestyle that the person was born into. A break in any other line can be seen as disruptive, but on the Life Line it can indicate a complete change in life, such as a new career or home. It is the only line that reveals the possibility of emigration, also seen as a break in the Line. The Life Line will always give information regarding a person's physical constitution and strength as well as the probable course a life will take.

93

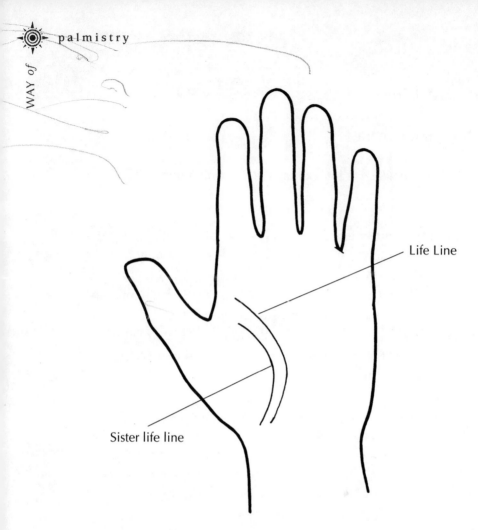

Life Line

Sister life line

Figure 11: The Life Line and the Sister Life Line

What to Look For

The Line of Life begins at the side of the hand between the index finger and the thumb and runs down towards the wrist ending below the thumb. The Line surrounds and outlines the mount of Venus, the fleshy pad at the base of the thumb (Chapter 17).

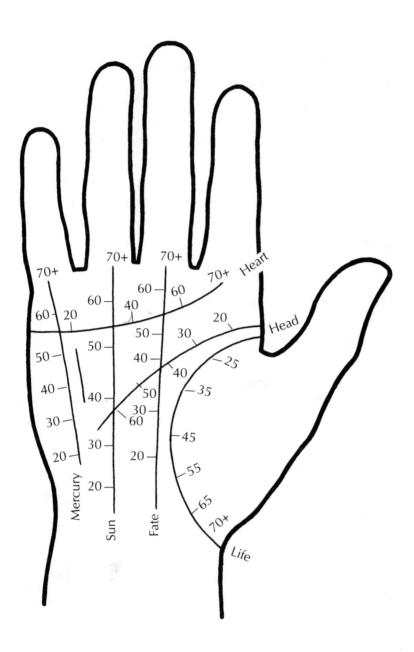

Figure 12: Major Lines Time Gauge

What we are looking for is a good clear line, preferably with no other lines crossing it, and no gaps or adverse marking. The firmer and wider the sweep of this Line the more vitality and zest for living is implied. It also shows that the person will move away from their childhood environment. They are not destined to chat over the garden fence, living next door to mother. The closer the Life Line hugs the base of the thumb, the less adventurous the owner will be. If the Life Line is free from all other fine lines crossing it this eliminates the possibility of interference from outside forces, and it shows a fortunate life with a sound constitution. A poor, thin, broken, or frayed-looking line shows a tendency to bad health, and a lack of stamina leading to a mediocre existence.

The Three Sections of the Life Line

The Starting Section – 25 to 50 Years
The Life Line starts at the side of the palm, generally three quarters of an inch below the index finger. When a person has a poor start in life it will show on the Line as many islands, chaining with a weak appearance. Such a commencement indicates childhood difficulties. Also at the beginning of the Life Line is recorded our relationship with our parents from birth onwards and early experiences in the world. If the Life Line seems to emerge from a circle at its starting point, and the Line continues on and is broken in places, it indicates some mystery attached to the birth. May indicate illegitimacy or a difficult birthing.

Mid-Life Section – 25 to 50 Years
What to look for generally in this period is for a well-shaped arch forming a regular course. This denotes the ability to look at life objectively, assessing the positive and negative aspects calmly and sensibly. When the Line clings closely to the thumb it is known as

the narrow Life Line, the indication being a less eventful life experience – a person of caution and stability. Although the adult life may
be less interesting there are many compensations for the consistency of an ordinary life. Any little lines attached to the Life Line,
pointing upwards, refer to some help given at those particular times
to further ambitions. Any lines going across the main Life Line indicate family influences upon the person. If the Life Line crosses way
over the palm to the middle of the hand or beyond, it shows a very
adventurous life, the grass certainly will not grow under that person's feet. Travelling will also be a key factor to achieving their goal.
They will strive constantly for personal freedom

The End Section – 50 to 70 Years

The longer the Line continues down the hand in a strong clear manner, the better the health will be.

It shows that the person has continuing vitality and zest even in the
declining years. Lots of small lines or fraying at the end reveals a
general weakness mentally and physically as one progresses into
death. It is wise to remember that to be able to record these lines at
all means they must still be alive! Armed with this knowledge they
can always change events for the better: perhaps improve the diet
or take additional exercise to relieve stress.

A Life Line that ends under the mount of Venus and curves around
the ball of the thumb, shows that the person will not travel far. They
will always like to be on home ground, even if they are interested in
reading about exotic places. When the Life Line ends far across the
palm heading towards the Lunar Mount, especially on the active
palm of Now, then the person is an adventurer and is not destined
for a conventional routine existence.

Minor Lines Attached to the Life Line – Positive

All short lines that are attached to the Life Line and are pointing upwards toward the top of the palm, give a great uplift to the person and bring optimism and the will to overcome at the time their departure is seen from the main Line. A very positive boost and support.

Minor Lines Attached to the Life Line – Negative

Any lines leading off from the main Life Line that point downwards toward the base of the palm or the wrists, show signs of strain and adversity at the times indicated by their departure from the main Line.

The Short Life Line Myth

Perfect Life Lines are few and far between. In reality the Life Line is the one that shows the most variations, because of experiences that we have had or are likely to encounter along the way. It is understood that you cannot have too long a Life Line, so the belief is the shorter the Life Line, the shorter the life. Although appearing to be short, the Life Line may still be sustained by a good Head Line or a strong top end of the thumb. In other words, look elsewhere to back up the short Life Line. A strong willpower, which is seen in a positive Head Line, can support and uplift, and has been known to sustain life in an otherwise debilitated body. The Head Line and thumb will support the person's fight against a physical weakness or an abrupt ending which might otherwise cause his death if not energetically resisted. A short Life Line can also mean that the person has ceased to make any real effort from the time the Line ends, and is content to just sit life out.

The Wavy Life Line

It is unusual to see a Life Line that zig zags across the palm. If it does, then look to the timing of its curves, where it changes direction, which will indicate precisely the incredible changes that are likely to be coming in. When the Line continues after the curves then the person still remains on the same course as before, but will have to adapt to changed circumstances. If there is a break in the Line the person's direction will have to be totally reorganized before they can continue. A U-turn will have taken place.

Timing of Events

The timing for the Life Line is started at the place it connects to the Head Line underneath the index finger before the Jupiter mount, and ends as it curves in towards the base of the thumb. This span covers roughly seventy years, which is the original three- score years and ten. As we have a longer life span today, the Line could cover 80 years. Use a piece of white cotton and lay it around the length of the Line. Fold it in two and mark it with a pen and place it back on the Life Line curve. This will give the halfway life-expectancy position.

Starting Positions of the Life Line

The Life Line Starting on the Mount of Jupiter

When the Life Line starts on the mount of Jupiter, which puts it slightly above the Head Line, it shows that the person was born with a burning desire to succeed. They are full of ambition and prepared to tackle anything that will lead them along the road to success. They become the leader of the pack.

The Life Line Starting on the Mount of Mars

The Mars Mount is the mount just below the start of the Life Line. Whether it is a promising start or not depends on the size of the Mars mount. If the mount is normal sized, then the person will have a confident start, full of enthusiasm and ambition. If it starts on a flat mount, the person will lack confidence and be slightly reticent and always a bit unsure about life. A very large Mars mount will give the person a start in life that is rather inclined to be aggressive and self-possessed, totally driven by ambition, impulsive, extroverted, and reckless.

The Life Line Starting Connected to the Head Line

The Life Line can be attached at its beginning to the Head Line. If so, there will be a restriction in the subject's childhood – parental authority will be strong. A careful, cautious nature is indicated – they think before they act. Where the Life Line eventually breaks away from the Head Line shows the age that the person becomes independent from the family. The longer the Lines are connected the more difficult it is for the person to make decisions on their own.

The Ending Positions of the Life Line

The Positive Life Line Ending

Any Life Line that ends strongly on its own, and with no adverse markings, shows that the person will be fully active all their days. Any fine lines that touch the Life Line coming from the Line of Fate, will also give added support and help wherever it touches. If the Fate Line connects to the end of the Life Line, it is truly fortunate.

The Pronged-Fork Life Line Ending

When the Life Line ends with a fork, especially a two-pronged fork, it shows that the owner will be restless and indecisive in their old age.

The Frayed Life Line Ending

The end of the Life Line can have many small lines or fraying, giving the appearance of a tassel. This reveals a general weakness in health as one progresses into death.

The Crossed Life Line Ending

The Life Line may have a series of crosses located at the end of the Line. Four or more crosses placed close together indicates that despite the person doing quite well in life earlier on, the person will not have the tranquil senior years that they anticipated.

The Depth and Furrowing of the Life Line

How deep a line is etched into the palm can be gauged from the information below:

Medium Depth Line A line appears medium deep when you can put the tip of your nail into the line. It is the most desired depth of a line.

The Shallow Line A shallow line skims lightly over the surface of the palm tracing a thin line. It appears wispy and can be difficult to see. This diminishes the line's strength and characteristics.

Shallowness of the Life Line indicates, in the area that it is present, periods of low activity and a moody temperament, when things are easily put off. Some parts may be shallower than the rest of the Line, showing contraction periods when the person is taking stock. These are reassembling times before pushing onwards again.

The Deep Line A deep line occurs when it is a definite crevice, so that the point of a knife will sink into the line for about an eighth of an inch. The deeper the line the brusquer and pushier the personality.

If the Life Line appears much deeper than the rest of the lines on the hand, then it is an indication of deep resentment and anger which usually causes havoc with the constitution, work and relationships. Where it varies in depth along the Line the deeper parts can represent activity and moving forward.

Width The wider a line spreads itself out, the larger-than-life the attributes will appear, according to that particular line.

In good health the Life Line should be medium in width. If it is too wide it becomes like a river that over-runs its bank. The person squanders their talents because of exhaustion.

Colour

The Life Line wears the Red Badge of Courage.

The colour meanings I have given for the lines on the palm are essential if you want to get a fuller understanding both emotionally and physically. These aspects are usually ignored by most palmists, but they always played a major role in the interpretation of the hand, both professionally and for the layman, centuries back.

Remember, the clearer the lines on the hand, free from shadow or dark markings, the better. Look for a nice healthy-looking medium-pink colour.

Pink A pink colour of the Life Line is considered to be normal and healthy when it is not vividly different or distinct from the general colour from the rest of the hand.

Pale Paleness of the Line indicates ill health because of poverty of the blood. The lymphatic system is sluggish. A feeble and envious character.

White A white Life Line usually suggests circulatory problems. There is a weakness in the constitution, with a lack of purpose. Not a good mixer.

Yellow A tendency towards liver problems or anything associated with the digestion. A yellow tinge to the Life Line shows a sad, difficult existence. Life is disrupted by outside events.

Blue A cold disposition. Emotionally unmoved, but a deep thinker. Needs physical exercise. Look for any heart conditions.

Red A strong red Life Line means a need for excitement and adventure with the ambition and energy to attain it. Can be over-anxious. Must watch stress and strain.

Very dark red on a pale-coloured palm indicates inner conflict.

Deep red The darker red the Life Line is, the more dogmatic and controlling the personality. Must win at all costs. Quick tempered, could be violent or brutal.

Positive Aspects of the Life Line
Zest. Energy. Drive. Go for it. The Pioneers. Power. Courage. Creativity. Perseverance. Cheerfulness. Rescuer. Dynamic. Reviver. Stability.

Negative Aspects of the Life Line
Intolerant. Destructive. Warmonger. Bully. Graceless. Shame. Guilt. Stubborn. Ruthless.

Transformation

Each of the major lines gives a list of positive growth suggestions to enable the development of the best of the line's opportunities. Using their positive thoughts brings balance and harmony and can transform what may appear to be an undesirable line into a positive one.

This section covers the 'where do I go from here' area in Palmistry, once the information available has been gathered from the hand's features. How do you deal with what you find, addressing luck, seemingly good or negative fortune, fate and destiny. The transformation suggestions give some personal growth pointers towards positive goal setting and strategies to go with the information revealed by that specific line.

Transformation of the Life Line

- All that had transpired in your life had been designed to bring you to this moment – and the next and the next ...
- Remember this life that you are living now is no dress rehearsal – this is it – go for it now. Seize the day always.
- Our life is what our thought makes of it.
- Each day is a new beginning, the first day of the rest of your life.
- Move forward and start to own your real power and true identity.
- Start gardening – grow some seed in pots indoors.
- Reassess your life, i.e. am I happy with my daily routine?
- Set new goals.

- Dare to take a risk – you cannot make an omelette without cracking eggs.
- Plan a holiday of a lifetime – and do it. Do it now.
- Make all those telephone calls to friends you keep meaning to do.
- Clear out all your unwanted clothes and cupboards and start afresh.
- Stand up for your rights – look to your hidden agenda.
- Welcome in changes and drink the elixir of fearlessness.
- You can only understand life by looking backwards but it has to be lived forwards.

Healing Meditation

At the end of each of the six major lines, a healing meditation is given harnessing the powerful vibration of colour. The Colour Healing Meditation section, using the art of visualization, is one of the most effective tools for clarifying desires and setting into motion the energy needed for creating an expectation of success. When you start to use the meditation, either for yourself or your clients, be aware of the characteristics of the line that it is connected to. If, for instance, you have just read the Life Line, then imagine or have your client imagine what changes are desired in the present day to day life style. If focusing on the Heart Line, concentration is on the person's ideal relationship. This makes new ideas ready to go to work immediately.

The colour used has been specifically chosen to harness the light's energy force, coupled with the power of your own positive thoughts. Having established the intention for a particular line, then go quietly into visualizing the Colour Healing Meditation.

This is a simple yet powerful way to heal and strengthen your Life Line, which in due course enhances your daily life and well being.

Close your eyes and visualize the top of your head opening and a beautiful scarlet red ray of light beaming down straight into your body. Feel this energizing vibration tingling through your being filling you up with strength and new vitality. Let it course through your veins singing with joy. Let this scarlet light shower you with its sparkling essence of rebirth so that you move forward to a new, fresh start in life. Take in a deep breath and exhale. Do this three times and then – RELAX.

The Sister Life Line

The Inner Line of Life

Sometimes there is another line running inside the Life Line on the mount of Venus. This is know as the 'Sister' Line or Double Life Line. Wherever it is visible it is a good sign, as it gives an extra boost and support to the Life Line. It may not run all the way along the Life Line, but may be segmented. Where it covers a weak patch in the Life Line it gives great protection at a shaky time. It lends physical stamina plus psychological support in the event of any difficulties, i.e. accidents or emotional traumas. It has double its strength if the Life Line also has any little upward side branches coming from it. This gives an extra lift.

THE HEAD
Line

*Knowledge is that which is left over after we have
forgotten what we were taught at school.*

ALBERT EINSTEIN

The Head Line is the next path to observe after the Life Line. It reveals our mental capacity and intellectual prowess. It is called the Head Line because it gives important information about the extent and depth of the subject's reasoning power. The memory and career potential is also shown along with the person's ability to fit into the outside world regarding people and situations. It is of no use having a splendid Life Line that indicates great promise only to be thwarted by a weak Head Line, suggesting there won't be the common sense to carry out life's opportunities. Unfortunately a weak Head Line can lead to the recipient withdrawing into themselves. The longer, stronger and straighter the Head Line, the more confidence there will be.

The Head Line concerns all matters connected to reasoning and measuring, giving more control over the self. It shows the common-sense attributes of the person. The perfect Head Line, which is slightly curved in the middle, is rare. The person with a perfect Head Line will be very clear about life. They have the ability to penetrate, lending a shrewdness of mind to business and money matters, whilst at the same time being capable of bringing in their imaginative powers.

If the Head Line appears weak, then look to the Mercury Line, also known as the Health or Liver Line. If it is well-placed then it will bring its own qualities to the Head Line to back up and support it. When the Liver is good, perfect digestion helps clarity of thought and brightens disposition. Also check to see if the top end of the thumb is strong and straight. This gives added willpower to the Head Line that contributes to a brilliant career in business.

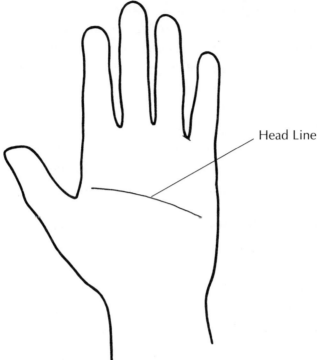

Head Line

Figure 13: The Head Line

What to Look For

The Head Line travels straight across the upper part of the palm, positioned below the Heart Line and above the Life Line. A good Head Line gently slopes down at the end of its run, ending with a small fork suggesting a good balance between imagination and logic if it is free of adverse marks such as black spots. The stronger the Line is the better the person is able to deal with life's ups and downs. Reason will prevail and intelligence will come to the fore. If a child shows a dominant Head Line they will be equipped to achieve academically. If the Line is delicate and wispy then their talents would be better directed towards the arts, or special care taken

109

WAY of

in explaining scientific subjects. It does not mean that the person is unintelligent, but that they are less inclined to have the emotional stamina to achieve. The pressure can cause mental stress and break-downs. Consideration and support must always be given with a delicate Head Line.

When the Head Line doesn't have a curve at all and just goes straight across the palm with no dipping down anywhere, then it shows the person has immense business acumen, great concentration powers and is very practical and determined.

Dividing the Head Line Into Three Sections

The Starting Section – Birth to 25 Years
The stronger the Head Line is at the beginning, the better the chance the person has to utilize their reasoning power later on. A solid-looking first section will usually create a longer Head Line later on. The longer the Head Line the more varied the person's interests are in life. Because they are capable of turning their hand to any-thing, life won't let them down. They are great opportunists. The belief is that if one area of their life doesn't work, they will change it. Abundance is the name of the game. As they work from the intel-lect, good up-front planning sees to it that they get it. The possessor of the long Head Line is always busy and likes to have lots of hob-bies. If the Line is very thick or broad at the beginning, the person will only be happy if they get their own way.

The Middle Section – 25 to 50 Years
If this middle part of the Line is free of black dots, islands and breaks then the person will have a relatively hassle-free adulthood. Life will treat them kindly. When the start of the Head Line shows promise and the middle section that follows is weak, then it shows

that they have not fulfilled their potential. This usually means they have not been fortunate enough to have an appropriate education. An inferiority complex has set in and lack of confidence follows. Usually outside forces have interrupted their ability to concentrate.

The End Section – 50 to 70 Years

The stronger the Line is in this third part, the less the likelihood of senility in the senior years. If the end of the Line slopes slightly down towards the wrist, then the person has a good imagination and will always bring creativity into their life. When it drops sharply down towards the wrist there will be a tendency towards living in a fantasy world, always making a mountain out of a molehill. If the downward section has any breaks in the Line or any black dots then depression could be a possibility. The intellect will also be poorly balanced.

Starting Positions of the Head Line

The Head Line Joined to the Life Line

If the Head Line starts joined with the Life Line, it shows that the individual's parents kept a tight rein on them as a child. The parents will have tried to force the child into the family footsteps. The point where the Head Line eventually separates from the Life Line shows the time the fledgling flew the nest. Anxiety and emotional problems in life distress this person unduly.

The Head Line Separated from the Life Line

When the Head Line is separated from the Life Line so that a gap between the two is noticeable, it means a rather lonely start to life. Parents were absent or did not involve themselves in the child's early life.

The Head Line Starting Inside the Life Line

The Head Line can start inside the Life Line, resulting in a rather tetchy temperament if the Mount of Mars that it starts on, is large. If the Mars Mount is flat it's likely the person will be a worrier. When this mount is a nice, round, normal size, there is the ability to face any challenges that may come one's way in life. As this lower Mount of Mars is also located at the top of the Venus Mount the person will be able to assert their charm in a most beguiling way.

The Head Line Starting on the Jupiter Mount

When the Head Line starts on the Jupiter Mount, located beneath the index finger, then the person is likely to be ambitious and very successful in life if the mount is of normal size. They have a very outgoing personality full of inspiration and leadership qualities. If the mount is exceptionally high and hard to the touch, then the person will have a tendency to be arrogant and domineering. A flat mount indicates a lack of confidence, which is a pity as there will be plenty of ideas, but they all get lost because of the lack of push.

The End of the Head Line

The Pronged-Fork Ending

The Head Line ending with a three-pronged fork shows combined intelligence, imagination and business ability.

The Split Dropped Ending

The Head Line splitting at the end with one part dropping downwards toward the top of the wrist and the top part going up to touch the Heart Line, shows that the person will give up everything for love.

Minor Line Attached to the Head Line

The Downward Line Leading off the Head Line

The Head Line showing a line leading off and diving down towards the wrist, indicates at the time that it branches off from the Head Line, that the person needs to focus on one thing and not take on too many projects. Too much versatility can dissipate their talents.

Wavy Head Line

If the Head Line weaves from one direction to another, then watch out when this person is about. They will be extremely difficult to pin down, dithering, and lacking in concentration. It makes them Jack-of-all-trades and the master of none. The career will take twists and turns, and the path will not be smooth. May become the conman.

Short Head Line Myth

A short, small or ill formed Head Line always indicates a thwarted and unhappy life, including accidents or sudden illnesses. It is considered short if it ends abruptly on the Saturn mount under the middle finger. This is believed to result when the subject has encountered a mishap that has stopped the flow of his mental powers. The Life Line can balance this out – if the Life Line is long it will counteract the negativeness of a short Head Line. On the plus side, a short Head Line may indicate that the person realizes that they don't wish to continue the way they are, and a total change in life and a fresh start is possible – if they bother to do it.

The Timing of Events

To gauge the events of the Head Line, start at the thumb end and work across the palm to the edge of the hands. This Line originally spanned seventy years, but you can increase it to eighty. Measure the Line and take the centre point to indicate forty years. Another method of midway pinpointing is to use the gap that separates the fingers into two sets of two. This is the space between the middle and third finger or the Saturn and Apollo fingers; the midpoint will fall directly below it.

The Depth and Furrowing of the Head Line

Shallow The thinner the Head Line the quicker the mind. They will not hang around and stagnate; the tendency is to keep moving, suggesting the mental talent could be used as a dancer or sportsman. Must be careful not to make errors. Has a quicksilver tongue. Should never risk burning the candle at both ends as the mental strength should be conserved.

Deep When the Head Line has a depth to it then the person knows their own mind. Prefers reality to fantasy. Self-esteem will be high. A deeper thinker. The scientist. Can be absent minded.

Width When the Head Line spreads out and becomes wide, it can show a tendency to laziness. Sometimes overrides sense for cleverness. Lots of irons in the fire but unable to follow through.

Colour of the Head Line

The Head Line wears the Yellow Badge of Intellect.

Pink A nice rosy pink is the most desirable hue for the Head Line, giving an even temperament and sound judgement.

Pale When it becomes pale it shows a lack of energy, leading to a dull intellect. Low powers of concentration. The person tires easily. Must get plenty of rest and sleep.

White Any white spots on the Line indicate great excitement, good luck and fortune at those times. The person will have success in their careers, particularly in the sciences.

Yellow This is the only Line on the palm where a yellow colour does not necessarily mean digestive problems. The yellow tinge only enhances the mind and brain power.

Blue A blue tinge to the Head Line belongs to the philosophical thinker. Strong ability to concentrate. May appear close and quiet as individuals, but don't be misled by their cool nature. Still waters run deep.

Red The great pioneers and pushers in life, particularly in business. If they say they are going to do it, they will. Great get up and go.

Dark red Cruel bully tendencies. Gains satisfaction at the expense of others.

Black If there are black marks or spots on the Line, reasoning powers will be diminished at those times because of hindrances, both from outside and self-inflicted.

Positive Aspects of the Head Line
Quickness of mind. Optimistic. Tenacious. Loves new ideas. Diplomatic. Scintillating talker. Inquisitive. Broadminded. Loves to laugh. Domestic. Slim. The great networker.

Negative Aspects of the Head Line
Evasive. Lazy. Fat. Criminal. Callous Dictator. Mental collapse. Restless. Exhausting. Sarcastic. Foolish. Doesn't always get priorities right.

Transformation of the Head Line

It is not because things are difficult that we do not dare, it is because we do not dare that they are difficult.

- Make a five-year plan: structure your life and be clear about your intentions.
- Get a computer. Got one? Then take ballet lessons instead.
- Read those books you've always wanted to.
- Write articles and send them to publishers.
- Mind power means me power.
- Start saying, I know instead of I think so.
- Learn a language.
- Within the next six weeks earn yourself money as a street entertainer – singing – dancing.
- Check your bank accounts – learn business acumen.
- Make a will or update the one you have got.
- Women: grasp how to change a fuse or the wheel of a car.
- Men: grasp how to cook and wash and iron.
- One door shuts and another one opens.
- What doesn't kill me makes me stronger.
- Sell your cleverness and buy bewilderment.
- Throw out all unwanted paper – clear your files.
- Learn the art of active listening.
- See all – hear all – say what suits you.
- The self is the home-base for the mind.

Healing Meditation

As a man thinks about himself he sooner or later discovers that he is the master gardener of his soul.

Close your eyes and visualize the top of your head opening and a beautiful brilliant yellow light beaming straight down into your body. Let it filter through your mind clearing away any stress or strain. Allow your mind to become still and quiet whilst bathed in this shimmering beam of sunlight. Take in a deep breath and exhale. Do this three times and RELAX.

ELEVEN

THE

Heart Line

Love becomes the ultimate answer to the ultimate question.

ARCHIBALD MACLEISH

Our Heart Line represents our emotional life, and is known as the curve of creativity. Its importance is in its role as a guide to individual emotions and the way they are experienced. It shows if a person is warm-hearted and giving or introverted and cold. Studying the Heart Line highlights the many facets of love. Each person's approach to love and relationships is unique and private, but the pattern that the Heart Line shows can help define the needs and expectations the individual desires. This Line is the most variable of all because its main task is to record information about affairs of the heart. It is particularly important to observe the markings on the Heart Line as they may be many and varied. Emotions fluctuate and wane continually, as they are the experiences of our creative self; this in turn will lead to many markings appearing on the Line, such as breaks, chaining, etc. Understanding this Line gives many clues regarding compatibility in relationships. If a couple both possess a fragmented, highly emotive Heart Line they may experience difficulty in their partnership – but it certainly won't be boring!

A long, straight Line running across the palm nearly always indicates a coldness in the person's temperament. They like to remain in a relationship; consistency is the name of the game. Demanding in their need for relationships, they are nonetheless unable to enjoy the love game.

The Heart Line records both emotional states of being and the condition of the physical pump. We can expect to see recorded conditions related to heart ailments and diseases, and heart attack. Emotional breakdowns caused by fear and fatigue will be recorded

119

on the Line by numerous fragmented smaller hair-lines coming off the main Line.

The Heart Line should be read in conjunction with the Head Line in order that balance between emotions and interests can be clearly discerned.

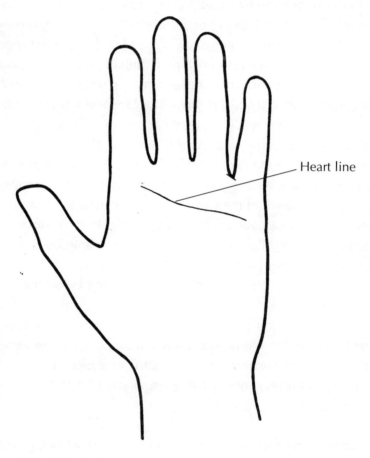

Heart line

Figure 14: The Heart Line

What to Look For

This is the only Line where palmists differ as to which end is the starting end. The author's long experience is that it should be read from the Mercury Mount. This Line is located at the top of the palm, roughly parallel to the Head Line but nearer the fingers. It starts at the base of the Mercury Mount, which is under the little finger, and continues straight across the hand, usually ending in a curve finishing in the middle of the Jupiter mount. This is a perfect Heart Line, which is, needless to say, very rare.

Dividing the Heart Line into Three Sections

The Starting Section – Birth to 25 Years

The ideal start to a Heart Line is a smooth, good-coloured Line free from any islands, black dots and breaks. If the child was unhappy it will be recorded in detail at the beginning of the Heart Line. The actual circumstances that caused the unfortunate emotional upsets will be recorded on the Life Line.

When the Heart Line starts high up, curving around the Mercury Mount, it can show a talent for the mystic arts. It is a much desired placement as it foretells the happiest of natures. But watch out for anyone whose Head, Heart and Life Lines are joined together at the beginning of the Life Line: they will usually stop at nothing to acquire their own aim.

The Middle Section – 25 to 50 Years

This section usually shows the most happenings on the Heart Line, as that is when we are most active in our love-life. The deeper the Line is at this stage the more able the person is to enjoy the purely physical aspects of love.

121

Islands on the middle section are always a weakening sign, showing a disposition to illness and heart problems. The indications are usually of emotional strain during that period. They should keep a close check on their health and keep fit.

The End Section – 50 to 70 Years

A descending Line of the Heart, where the end dips down toward the beginning of the Head Line, reveals a jealous nature, possessive in relationships. They also dislike poverty – don't ask this person out for a sandwich, and wear jeans on your first date. They like wining and dining in luxury.

When the end of the Heart Line branches into three lines, this is a good marking signifying a balance between the emotions, common sense and physical pleasure. This is a good ending to any Heart Line. If the middle branch of the Line ends between the index and third finger, it shows we will emotionally attain that partner we have been looking for.

The Short Heart Line Myth

The Heart Line is considered short when, taking the edge of the palm as the start of the Line, it does not extend beyond the middle of the palm. A short Heart Line shows that somewhere in the person's life they experienced a disappointment with the emotions and feelings which won't allow them to be vulnerable again. The shorter it is the less interested a person is in intimacy, and they won't like the confines that a relationship can impose.

The *fear* of a short Heart Line is (a) the possibility of heart attacks or (b) of never finding that loved one. Both can be avoided. Keep fit, exercise, and keep the weight down to avoid heart problems. Finding that loved one will require a little extra input – staying at home looking at four walls won't find them. You have to speculate to accumulate.

The Wavy Heart Line

When the Heart Line weaves about it indicates the emotions will be a little haywire, according to the degree of the twists and turns of the Lines. Consistency will be a problem in relationships, but they will draw the opposite sex to them because of their unpredictable fantasizing, which is extremely alluring.

The Timing of Events

Timing for the Heart Line is a little different from the other lines as it can be done in two ways. The modern way to read this Line is to start counting from the Mercury end. Centuries back the timing was started from the index finger going towards the little or Mercury finger. Choose whichever one feels right or works for you. Both are correct. If you choose the latter one it will require you to use your psychic ability rather than your measuring capacity. As the Line spans 70 years, the midway mark of 35 years will be the point beneath the centre of the third finger.

Starting Positions of the Heart Line

The Heart Line Starting on the Mount of Mercury

The romantic talker will have a Heart Line starting here. They have the gift of whispering sweet nothings in your ear. The charming lover.

The Heart Line Starting Between the Mount of Mercury and the Upper Passive Mount of Mars

With the Heart Line beginning here, the person will have a well-balanced approach to relationships. They will feel quite comfortable with the opposite sex.

123

The Heart Line Starting Between the Mount of Jupiter and the Lower Active Mount of Mars

The Heart Line starting on this position will be inclined to keep their emotions in check. They will take time before committing themselves to a relationship. Although slow to get going in the emotional area, once smitten their passionate nature emerges.

The Ending Positions for the Heart Line

It is important to observe where the Heart Line ends as particular understandings can be gained from this. To gain more information just look up those fingers that the Line ends upon or near, and incorporate their meanings to get a fuller picture of the emotional character of the Line. An important point in considering the significance of the Heart Line is the extent of the curvature. The more curved it is the stronger the need for love and affection. The straighter the Line the less the need.

The information below applies when using the Mercury end of the Heart Line as the starting point.

The Heart Line Ending Under the First Finger

If the Line ends touching the base of the first finger on its inside edge, then this is the truest indicator that the person will eventually acquire the relationship they desire.

The Heart Line Ending Between the Index and Middle Finger

The person tends to take an idealistic view of love and marriage. Very enthusiastic but usually without practical application. Capable of strong emotion but may find disappointment as the partner may not live up to expectations. May eventually get what they want but could sacrifice much of their personality in the process.

The Heart Line Ending Near or Under the Middle Finger

Generally the person will show quite a balanced attitude towards the emotions. A tendency toward a lack of depth of feelings, but any upsets caused because of this would be short lived. May place work before personal needs, resulting in 'you in your corner and me in mine' attitude to relationships.

The Heart Line Ending Under the Third Finger

To have such a short Heart Line is quite common. The person may have some serious problems initiating and maintaining relationships. This Line stricture could also indicate that the person has decided to forego pleasures of the heart for more serious spiritual matters and a need for solitude.

The Depth and Furrowing of the Heart Line

Shallow A shallow Heart Line represents people who only need a little bit of attention and occasional affection. They will not be demonstrative in their show of emotions; the material side of life concerns them more. They would rather avoid intense feelings. This thin, stretchy Line likes to keep it light hearted – heavy affairs are not for them.

Deep The deeper the Heart Line is, the more love they wish to receive from their relationship encounters. The deep Heart Line shows that they are capable of rich emotional feelings. The catch is, they will expect the same back from their partners.

Width A wide Heart Line that spreads out, shows that the person is easily led by others. Falls for the sob story. Over exposed to other's feelings. Would rather save the world than their own marriage.

Colour of the Heart Line

The Heart Line wears the Green Badge of Relationships.

Pink The most desirable tint for the Heart Line is a medium pink. It indicates a balanced emotional approach to life. Healthy love instincts. Makes for a good reliable partner who is sensitive and capable of intimacy in relationships.

Pale A pale coloured Heart Line implies temporary or permanent sickness of the heart either emotionally, physically or maybe both. A tendency towards coldness. Low sexual urges. A fear of surrendering. Does not have a high regard towards the opposite sex. Impotence and frigidity.

White If there are white spots on the Heart Line, it will bring in a great love affair.

Yellow Self-denial in the sexual area. A leaning towards jealousy and a mistrust of relationships. Could be sick to the stomach because of the love-life situation. May be a gold digger, gigolo or very flighty.

Blue Best to consult your doctor just to check all is well with the heart, particularly if accompanied by blue nails and blue-tinged lips. It is unusual to see a blue Heart Line nowadays due to the expert care that we receive from birth.

Red A red Heart Line indicates a passionate personality. Look to see if the red appears only at certain patches along the Line, and then check the timing for these. A good love life can be expected at these times. A Heart Line that is obviously bright red compared to the rest of the hand, suggests too strong a sex drive, and a tendency to become a little rough, excluding romance.

Dark black-red This is not a desired shade to have on the Heart Line, as its possessor veers toward violence in love and sex.

Positive Aspects of the Heart Line

Open hearted. Productive. Balanced relationships. The ability to experience wholeness. Heart to heart linking. The matchmaker.

Negative Aspects of the Heart Line

Jealousy. Envy. Promiscuous sex. Rather be admired than loved. Gives loving at the expense of the self. Love starvation. Emotional upheavals. Conflict of emotions. Adultery. Desire disorders

Transformation of the Heart Line

We don't believe in rheumatism and true love
until after the first attack.
Marie Ebneroon Eschenback (1830–1916)

- No relationship is a failure. It just teaches you how not to do it next time.
- Breaking bonds requires energy. Making up bonds releases energy.
- Laugh at love.
- Write a love letter to yourself that you would love to receive.
- Write a love letter to an ideal mate you would love to meet.
- In a relationship always arrive where you both can win.
- Sex is the most fun you'll ever get without laughing.
- Look for romance within your own male and female-ness.

- Check the quality of your health. A healthy body is capable of maintaining a relationship.
- Let go of old ties that bind you.
- Put yourself into a space of relationship.
- Check what you've got – what you would like – what will come.
- Let love hold you together. It is the adhesive glue that keeps the universe connected.
- Shed the extra weight – skinnies round up a bit!
- Empowerment is holding the space for the *other* to show up in.
- Send yourself flowers.
- Be conscience that every act performed has its measure of love in it.
- Hugs are better than chocolate.
- Never value anything beyond its value.
- Practise skin cuddling.
- Make sure that you are not at the end of someone else's life.
- Don't be love sick – be love healthy.

Healing Meditation

Close your eyes and visualize the top of your head opening and a beautiful emerald light beaming down straight into your body. Allow this energy to filter through to your heart so that it becomes full. Let it flow over the heart and feel it spread across the whole of the chest area. Be conscious of the healing, soothing effect it has on your heart. Take a deep breath in and exhale. Do this three times and then RELAX.

Girdle of Venus

The Sister Heart Line

This Line runs in a semi-circle usually, from under the end of the middle finger (Saturn) and scoops down forming a loop ending up underneath the third finger (Apollo).

Not all hands possess this curved Line and it isn't necessary or essential but to have one. If present, this Line shows extreme sensitivity, and a sensuous personality with a magnetic nature. This Line is often made up of many very fine lines. The finer they are the more hypersensitive the personality; may be bordering on hysteria if the rest of the palm is weak. It is very fortunate if there appear to be two to three smooth lines that make up this girdle, suggesting good health and a strong temperament.

If the Line spans from the index finger (Jupiter) and ends by the small finger (Mercury) then the better the balance between the heart and head. This Line has been subject to misconception as in the past it was regarded as a sign of immorality and adultery. The owner was considered inconsistent in their love life. Men with such a girdle regarded it as a sign of their virility and welcomed it. Women feared it if it appeared in their partner's palm, as he could be a two-timer, always having a roving eye for the ladies. In women it was undesirable, regarded as flirtatious with an unstable temperament. Since the sexual revolution, it now reads the same for both sexes.

Many hands possess the girdle of Venus. It need only be of concern if the hand is square and very coarse, and if the Line is dark red in colour without any breaks in it. The owner of such a girdle will show a tendency towards obsessiveness and physical depravity.

129

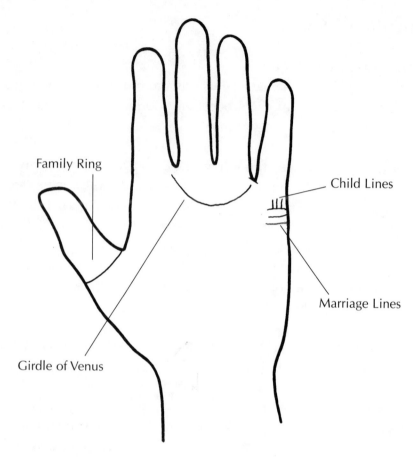

Figure 15: The Girdle of Venus

Ordinarily the girdle of Venus can only enhance romantic ardour and enthusiasm for life.

Minor Lines Relating to the Heart Line

To get a clearer understanding of these minor lines relating to our emotions, always refer back to the major Heart Line as its quality will strengthen the effect of the minor lines. For example, the Family

Ring may appear quite strong, but if the major Heart Line is generally weak, and faintly sketched in the palm, then it will dissipate some of the Ring's positive effects.

Compatability

For compatibility with a partner check two areas (a) the quality of the Heart Line itself, and (b) the basic shape of the hands. The shape reveals the basic temperament and personality and lays a foundation for compatibility analysis by a comparison of the personality traits for each hand-shape. Both partners with psychic hand shapes, for example, won't get much done in the material world. They will have lovely trips together away with the fairies romanticizing, but will find the bills piling up. A mutual tendency to over-sensitivity could prove problematical. A partnership where both people have square-shaped hands would experience an orderly life, without much excitement or fun between them. If accompanied by a rigid, stiff thumb a dictatorial state could ensue in the relationship.

Sex

Sex, the most important ingredient in a healthy, whole-hearted, committed relationship, can be gauged for compatibility by looking at the Venus Mounts on both person's hands. If one partner's Venus Mount is much larger than the other person's, then their sexual energies will differ. The higher mount indicates a stronger sex drive, which could prove to be a problem. *How many times a week* could prove an issue. It is best to have the mounts similar in their size and roundness, indicating a well-matched sexuality. It also helps to have a similar length of the Heart Line.

People with a reddish colour to their nails also seem to have a stronger sex drive, and are able to express their passions more easily.

131

The Reproductive System

The possibility of problems or weaknesses in the reproductive system of both sexes can be seen by the shape of the top Rascette (Chapter 15) that lies just below the base of the palm. If it has a curved shape then it would be wise to keep a check on this area. The more the arch moves up onto the palm the stronger the tendencies for menstrual or erection problems.

There is a marking that I have called the *flag* that sometimes accompanies the arch. It is attached to the Life Line halfway up the palm above the curve of the top Rascette and confirms the predisposition to prostate in men and prolapse in women, plus urinary problems that may not occur until post-menopause for both sexes.

The Family Ring

This line can be found at the base of the thumb at the end of the thumb's second phalange (Chapter 4). When it is chained and thick the person will have many family ties and commitments. The weaker the Line the fewer the family links. No Line at all indicates the person has broken all family ties or never really had much of a home life in the first place.

Family Influence Lines

These lines travel from the family ring across the Venus Mount. If they touch the Life Line it shows the family influenced the person's outlook considerably. If they fall short of the Life Line, relatives and friends tried to direct the person but failed. When a line crosses the Life Line and continues across the palm, the indications and markings where it ends gives an indication of family influences. No Family Influence lines means that the person may have been orphaned or brought up by an institution or people other than the biological parents. It could also mean the home ties were poor.

Marriage Lines

The so-called Marriage Lines are actually Lines of Union. They indicate the potential for an important relationship in a person's life, and the age at which it will occur. Even if the Line does not lead to marriage, it is clear that a relationship will make a profound impression upon the person at that time.

What to Look For

The Lines of Union are located at the side of the palm's edge, called the percussion. They run around and are always above the beginning of the Heart Line, moving on to the Mercury Mount. They can stretch some way across onto this mount. The longer the Line the longer the relationship. Any forks, markings or splits on the Line can also be taken into account (Chapter 16). These Union Lines can also mean a non-sexual relationship, but mainly they point to a partnership in its fullest context.

What to look for in these Lines is a clear, straight, long, Line free of breaks and islands. The deeper the Line the more important the union. If the Line dips at the end then it shows that the quality of the relationship has tapered off. Always read the timing on the Union Lines from left to right. A fork at the end could mean a split or divorce, but the partners could stay together living in the same house but pursue their own lives in separate ways.

Children's Lines

Where and what the markings are for the so-called Children's Lines differ amongst palmists. In my experience I have found it most accurate to count the tiny horizontal lines moving upwards from the Lines of Union.

These Lines will only indicate the possibility of children. If contraception is used then of course the likelihood of them materializing is greatly diminished. Abortions will also be recorded as a 'line' of a child, but it will be diffused and wider-spread that the other child lines. If there are many children marked, particularly on the last Line of Union, it may not mean that the person will personally give birth to them all. Check whether the client is a school teacher or is involved in children's work. The child lines will be recorded on both men and women's hands.

Twins

If one of the children's lines splits into two at the end it could indicate the possibility of twins.

The Breakup of Relationships

Look at the Lines of Union to see if there are any breaks in them. Each break represents the splitting of a relationship at that time. When the breaks in the Lines overlap, it indicates a possibility that the couple will come together again.

Disappointment in Love

The Heart Line will give clues regarding whether an affair of the heart will be a disappointment. Any small, short lines that spring from the Line of the Heart and point downward toward the wrist, indicate a loss. But the possessor of these lines should not despair. It may well indicate the need to just work harder at relationships in the future.

When there is a line running horizontally that connects to both the Heart and Head Line, it means that the person had or will have a very traumatic relationship. The person will emerge stronger and wiser from the experience. The same mistakes will not be made again.

The Seducer/Seductress

The seducer has *many* small, fine horizontal lines running around the percussion side of the palm and across the Mercury Mount, beneath the fourth finger. Each one represents a short affair. This person cannot, perhaps surprisingly, be seriously considered a cheating heart. Their relationships never develop any depth or commitment during their inevitably short duration.

When Will I Find True Love?

Any lines that are attached to the Heart Line and point upward towards the fingers, indicate happy relationships. The point at which these lines are attached to the Heart Line give an indication of when these compatible loves will occur.

Love at First Sight

A star-marking (Chapter 16) occurring on the Heart Line will indicate when this 'instant attraction' is likely to turn up. Again, its positioning along the Line will give an indication of the timing.

TWELVE

THE
Fate Line

> *What we vividly imagine, ardently desire, enthusi-*
> *astically act upon, must inevitably come to pass.*
>
> COLIN P. SISSON.

The word 'fate' in this instance refers to your life's work and the daily happenings that you are exposed to, whether they are for good or ill. The Fate Line is also known as the Line of Saturn, as it usually ends under the base of the third finger, having started at the wrist. This Line gives information regarding career and work prospects. The stronger it is the greater the chance to achieve a decent standard of living as a result the goals we have set ourselves. This Line indicates whether the amateur can become a professional. Work plays a major role in our lives: having a satisfying, fulfilling career can make the difference between a boring humdrum existence, or an enhancing, self-evolving vocation. Work focuses us towards our reason for living, which provides the opportunities for personal growth. Parents and the early emotional environment play a major part in the shaping of this Line, as it also denotes our family relationships and duties. Quite often we were directed to a form of work that was our parent's idea of what we should do. It was not our choice, but theirs. It is difficult for a child to object against such authority. Protest one may well do, but ultimately the child needs to please its parents. The way this unfulfilled natural career potential can be seen on the Fate Line, is that it appears weak and sketchy. A brilliant accountant or doctor could show this Line depleted despite their sound working record, because what they were pushed into is not what they really wanted to do. This Line more than any other is the Line that shows the personal growth of the owner – learning to stand up for oneself and say no or yes from choice. A person working at what they really want to do, regardless of its so-called standing in society, is indeed *master* of his own fate.

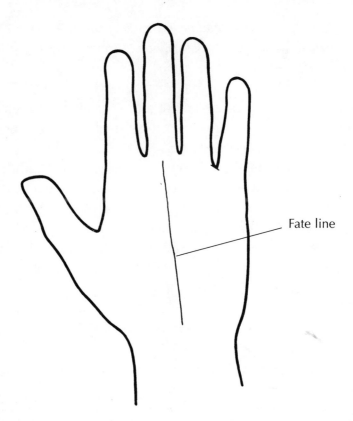

Fate line

Figure 16: The Fate Line

What to Look For

The Fate Line is located in the middle of the palm, usually running up in a vertical line from the base of the palm just above the wrist, heading towards the third finger. As stated, this Line has major implications for our work and career. When it runs full-length in a strong, unbroken Line and has no markings, it shows the person will have a secure career and working life with a minimum of problems. There is the possibility of staying in the same company and giving

loyal service until retirement. This is the same for both men and women. If the woman does not go out to work, it indicates a comfortable marriage, devoting her time to her family.

When the Line is broken in both partners, and the man is in a permanent job whilst his wife stays at home, then neither party will be happy with the conventional role where daddy earns the money and mummy stays at home. A compromise will have to be made if frustration and quarrels are to be avoided. In this case look to the Sun Line (Chapter 13). If it is strong, then there is a good chance that both will get what they want, when role-playing has been scrutinized and adjustments made.

If the Line is over-dominant in the hand then work loses its perspective. For many people their work compensates for their poor social life. It can be a means of escape from other problems or a difficult relationship.

A weak Fate Line that is barely etched on the palm, with fine lines or fragmented parts, indicates that the person hasn't found their role in life's work, especially in regard to service to their fellow men or the community. Restlessness and frustration are inevitable unless the person has decided not to work because they have an objection to the nine-to-five routine. This is fine provided they have private means or are adept at coping with the extreme hardships and poverty which the lack of funds often creates. If this is not the case and the person genuinely wants to find their niche or vocation, then extra direction and support will be needed to help that person find an interest that inspires them.

Dividing the Fate Line into Three Sections

The Starting Section – Birth to 25 Years

The beginning of the Fate Line for the first inch and a half depicts the early years. This is the period that covers the experimental time when the person is looking around to see what career or work to pursue. It can be the time of study once the person has decided which course to follow. The Line should be quite clear and unbroken. This section of the Fate Line does not as such record the family ties. For the early start with parents, look to the beginning of the Life and Head Lines. If the early section of this Line is missing in the adult's palm, it means that the child had no positive direction from their parents during the missing time-segment. A plain, uninterrupted start with a strong Line low down the palm near the wrist, shows the person has always had an idea of what they wanted to do. Many children express a desire to be a train driver or a nurse and they never waver; they appear to be the lucky ones who eventually achieve their childhood dream. The not-quite-sure group will have several fragmented lines at the start of the Fate Line. This shows they were constantly changing course and direction from one idea to another. When these early-launching lines eventually settle down into a single line then the person is on their way. Where this happens gives the timing for this occurrence. It's important to note in the under-15 year-old's palms if the Fate Line is absent. If so they will need support and guidance during this early period to enable them to focus on their future career direction.

The Middle Section – 25 to 50 Years

The mid-life section shows the building years of a person's life for both career and family fortunes. Between twenty and forty years is a time when a lot of changes can happen, and is the span where the physical effort is at its peak. The straighter and clearer the Line is at this mid-section, the more likely it is that the person has achieved the direction, purpose, and prosperity that puts the person in control of their endeavours. The forty-to-fifty year section also comes into this area of the Fate Line. This latter part can be a milestone for reviewing one's direction. Sometimes this section has a break in it, indicating a change of work and lifestyle. If the break overlaps itself there is no damage done – it can be a change for the better. When it's a total break, it could mean redundancy and hardship will occur for that amount of time.

The End Section – 50 to 70 Years

The end of the Fate Line focuses from the fifty age bracket to seventy-five plus. Quite often the Line starts to thin out at about this time and can stop altogether when the person's working years have come to an end. Fainter lines or several finer lines can often be seen coming off the main Line at this time, showing that the person has taken up several new interests and new hobbies.

A chain marking in the Fate Line as it crosses the Heart Line indicates trouble in the home life. When the end of the Fate Line continues on straight up the palm, ending at the base of the middle finger, then the person will keep working until the end of their days. This quite often happens when the person had found a new form of work at about fifty and opened up a career that stays with them though the 'retirement' period.

Short Fate Line Myth

The short Fate Line myth can be interpreted three ways. It can show that the person has come to a dead end in their working life and has given up because of disappointment. If this is the case then encouragement is needed to jump-start their enthusiasm again. The second understanding of a short Fate Line is that the person has been so successful that a very early retirement has occurred so that they can enjoy life to the full without financial worry. Lastly, a short or near absent Fate Line indicates strained family relationships that have become almost non-existent. Someone will have to make that first telephone call to break the ice if the tie is to survive.

Wavy Fate Line

When the Fate Line weaves from one side to the other, it can show a lack of purpose. The person will be hesitant and unable to be the master of their own ship of life. Focusing is required, otherwise the career will be constantly changing. Although the working life may not be a smooth and easy path, at least it won't be boring!

Timing of Events

To get the timing that the Fate Line reveals for career, life's work and a succession of happenings, fortunate or otherwise, find the beginning of the Line, which starts at the bottom of the palm near the wrist. The end of the Line will fall under the middle finger of Saturn. The timings on this Line are most important for gauging career changes and family events. The aspect of free will is an essential component of this Line so conscious effort upfront can alter any undesirable happening indicated.

The Starting Positions for the Fate Line

Where this Line of achievement starts is extremely important.

The Fate Line Starting from the Centre Palm

When the Line begins from middle of the wrist at the bottom of the palm and runs in a straight line up to the middle finger, it shows a no-nonsense independent type. They will keep their own council and are conscientious. A fortunate Line.

The Fate Line Starting from the Life Line

When the Fate Line is attached to the Line of Life at its beginning, it shows the person has strong family ties, and they will usually be late leaving home. This person works well in a group, and hates being alone. The Fate Line may eventually leave the Life Line, giving the time when they decided to flee the nest and stand on their own two feet.

The Fate Line Starting Inside Life Line

The Fate Line that starts inside the Life Line on the Venus Mount, shows that the person is indeed fortunate. The parents will have given their child both emotional and financial support, particularly if the Head Line is also strong.

The Fate Line Starting on the Lunar Mount

If the Fate Line begins on the Lunar Mount, the person will only be successful if they involve creativity in their career. The arts, media, design and any area of work that involves the public appeals to them. To be confined to an office with this placement of the Fate Line is akin to 'giving nuts to monkeys with no teeth'.

The Ending Positions for the Fate Lane

The Fate Line Ending on the Mount of Saturn

The usual place for the Fate Line to end is on the Saturn Mount which is just below the third finger. When the Line is strong and clear of any adverse markings the person has a chance to work well past their retirement age. Look further back on the Line to see if they have changed from perhaps a stressful career to work that is easier and which has enabled them to continue. The change can be seen by a crossover break in the Fate Line that slightly overlaps itself.

The Fate Line Ending on the Mount of Jupiter

When the Fate Line ends on the Mount of Jupiter, which is just below the index finger, it shows that the person has a wonderful chance to succeed in life because they are extremely ambitious.

The Fate Line Ending on the Mount of Apollo

The Fate Line ending on the Apollo Mount, under the third finger, generally indicates a career pursued in the field of the arts. This person will only be happy when using their creative flair.

The Fate Line Ending on the Mount of Mercury

If the Fate Line ends on the Mount of Mercury, which lies just below the fourth finger, it shows that the person has a very quick mind which does especially well in business because they are so versatile.

The Depth and Furrowing of the Fate Line

Shallow Whenever there is a shallow Fate Line, there will be a tendency to become stale and stuck in the work place and approach to life. They need to loosen up. The way to balance this is to encourage interests in the arts. Take up a creative hobby, go to the theatre. Don't let opportunities pass by for the sake of security.

Deep A deep Fate Line represents consciousness and the ability to focus. They have obviously mastered the ability to balance career and home life quite well. Watch out for a Fate Line that appears usually deep, as this can expose the bully. Unhappiness prevails here, as the person is likely to be in a profession they don't want to be in. Also indicates irritability.

Width When the Line is spread out too wide, the person will suffer from a lack of concentration. It will be extremely difficult for them to stick at any work. They will appear irresponsible, but it must be taken into account that they may never have been encouraged to develop and harness their business acumen. Childhood circumstances may have denied them the education they could have had.

Colour of the Fate Line

The Fate Line wears the Orange Badge of Opportunity.

Rose Pink This Line needs a very strong rosy hue to it to enable the person to forge ahead and take advantage of life's gifts, twists and turns.

Pale If the Line is pale in some parts compared to the rest of the lines, there will be problems ahead at those times. There will be no impetus, a lack of energy.

White A white-appearing line reveals a confused person, rigid in their outlook.

Yellow To see yellow on this Line is unfortunate, as it shows a weakness of willpower. Lack of confidence prevents the person from grasping opportunities. Fear of one's own shadow. Disappointment in life.

Blue A blue tinge indicates the person would rather find their vocation in quiet surroundings. Solitude is sought in regard to work. Careers in gardening or religion give that required.

Red A red Line of Fate shows single-mindedness and great zest, energy and drive. The person will get on because they have tenacity. Look to see if the whole Line is red, meaning it's go-for-it all the way. If it appears red at certain places only, those sections will indicate unusual spurts of progression work-wise.

Dark Black-red Dishonest dealings. Maybe prison. Gains money at the expense of others. Extortionist. Prostitution. The hard taskmaster.

Positive Aspects of the Fate Line
Achievement. Dynamic. Energy. Motivation. Mastery. Fulfilment. Loving Relationships. Integrated family life.

Negative Aspects of the Fate Line
Low self-esteem. Immobility. Workaholic. Guilt. Dictatorial. Lazy. Blocked. Self Defeating. Procrastination.

Transformation of the Fate Line

The people who get on in this world are the ones who get up and look for the circumstances they want and if they can't find them – make them.

- Self-definition starts with the inner circle – the family. Relatives are people too. Neither quarrel or give in, but understand the family and show that you want to help.
- Free yourself from expectations that others have of you.
- Get to grips with the dynamics of life.
- Every obstacle can be a stepping stone to success.
- Make a mistake – so what! Dust yourself down and start over again.
- Listen to the truth that is within you.
- Want things? Yes! But don't need them.

- Act. Do not react. Be the cause and not the effect.
- You are the inspirational force behind everything you do.
- It's not always what you know but whom you know, so start networking!
- Reassess your work skills.
- Deal with reality and not pie-in-the-sky thinking.
- Start to explore new ground – maybe relocate your work.
- The world is a stage so don't keep standing in the wings. Get out there and perform.
- Plan your time, it is essential. Reschedule and prioritize your commitments.
- Do not con others or yourself.
- Treat your partner's existence as a blessing.
- Stand fast – you can be shaken but not stirred.
- Achieve what you set out to do.
- Decide more consciously.
- To fall down is neither dangerous nor shameful but to remain lying down is both.

Healing Meditation

Whatever you can do or dream, you can begin it.
Boldness has genius, power and magic in it. Begin
it now.

GOETHE

Close your eyes and visualize the top of your head opening and a beautiful sunset-orange light beaming down straight into your body.

Feel this scintillating energy swirl through you, pulsating through every single cell. Let each particle of your body swell and expand in its gentle warmth. Experience a welling sensation of joyousness radiating from you, giving a supreme source of confidence and strength. Take a deep breath in and exhale. Do this three times and RELAX.

THIRTEEN

THE LINE OF
the Sun

*At the side of the everlasting Why?, there is a Yes
and a yes – YES!*

UNIVERSAL TRAINING

The Line of the Sun, or the Apollo Line as it is sometimes called, is considered to be the sister Line to the Line of Fate; a *second* Line of Fate. They are so closely related that the Sun Line boosts the Fate Line. Having a Sun Line in the first place is the problem! You may look at your hand and find that it seems to be non-existent. This shows that although you have financial security as seen on the Fate Line – even as far as the yacht and the private jet, you could still be unhappy. Do not dismiss the presence of this Line until you have used a magnifying glass, as it can appear as sketchy, fine lines.

The perfect Sun Line is long, without any breaks or adverse markings. A perfect Line indicates a contented existence through all stages of life. There is a great capacity for accomplishment.

Whenever this Line appears, it emphasizes personal success, fulfilment and happiness, as well as the capability to accomplish a great deal. A good strong Line of the Sun will always compensate for a weak Fate Line. In fact, the Line will boost the absence of any other line on the palm or if they appear delicate. The only time a strong Sun Line is diminished is when the thumb is weak (Chapter 4). Many well-known artists, actors, musicians and writers have a strong Line of the Sun. It shows a love of all the creative arts and things of beauty. The Sun/Apollo Line does not apply just to the arts, but to every type of daily activity.

This Line can also show the possibility of wealth without working – inherited money or perhaps winning the lottery. The possession of leisure is very fortunate. It's usually prosperity gained by some unusual talent. The bearer of a strong Sun Line is definitely creative and original, even bordering on genius, and can find success of the most complete kind.

It also symbolizes idyllic happiness and good fortune.

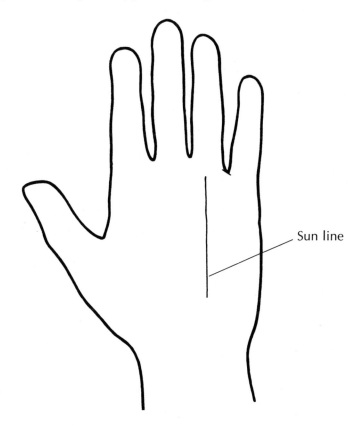

Sun line

Figure 17: The Line of the Sun

What to Look For

The Sun Line starts from the left-hand side of the palm when looking at the right hand, and visa versa on the left palm. It travels up from the wrist, to the third Finger of Apollo or the Sun finger. A long, prominent Line, free from adverse marks and from lines running across it, the greater the likelihood of riches coming in. It symbolizes happiness and good fortune. When this Line is short the prospects of accomplishing much are remote, no matter how clever or how talented the person. Achievements will occur only when the Line is present.

The first thing to look for is whether the Line is present or not. The person whose hands lack this vital Line may have all kinds of excellent qualities, but their life will be lived unrecognized. Effort and merit will go unrewarded. This will not mean a complete lack of success or that the person is a failure. It will indicate, however, that extra hard work is necessary to gain one's just desserts and a happier life. Remember lines can appear and disappear. A change of attitude is definitely required to bring this Line into the palm, to understand that you don't always have to struggle to get what you want.

When looking through a magnifying glass with a bright light, a weak Sun Line may appear as a very fine sketchy line or several little lines. They still constitute a Sun Line although in a diminished form. Many palms do not show this Line until halfway up the hand, which indicates that one gets the recognition one deserves in the second half of life.

Some believe that this Line means only the attainment of riches and power, but a person can be just as content with a so-called ordinary job. If the person is happy in whatever they do, then they conduct themselves in a manner that not only works but also earns admiration and respect from all those around them.

Dividing the Sun Line into Three Sections

The Starting Section – Birth to 25 Years

To have this Line starting strongly from the bottom of the palm, beginning by the wrist, is extremely fortunate. It shows there is a good chance for personal success, fulfilment and happiness, at least from childhood to 25 years. The continuation of this positive start will depend on whether the Line carries on up the palm. If not it could indicate a very promising start with lots of environmental support. It could show a child star or prodigy, only to be spent or burnt out after the teens. Pioneers often have this early Sun Line showing, as from childhood they will be preparing for their work later on. If the pioneer's Sun Line continues on up, then they do it!

The Middle Section – 25 to 50 Years

If the Sun Line is absent from the palm at this section, this indicates extreme bad luck as the person's projects and plans have come to nothing. Unforeseen obstacles have blocked the person's progress causing unfulfilled ambition. The person can overcome this if the last section of the Sun Line appears again, which shows good fortune returning. If the Sun Line doesn't continue at all beyond this point, it can indicate that the person has decided to opt out of the rat race or maybe they have inherited means but are not fulfilled emotionally as individuals.

The End Section – 50 to 70 Years

When the Sun Line rises from and above the Heart Line near the end of the palm, this is an especially fortunate sign, even if it hasn't shown up until now. The person may have experienced earlier in life a struggle financially, but somehow they will always have been rescued at the last moment, something would always turn up when they really needed it. Although it isn't likely that they will become mega-rich, they can rest assured they will never be without. A comfortable retirement to look forward to without struggle.

The Absent Sun Line Myth

The myth about this Line is the absence of any line at all. Usually this is associated with doom and gloom – a life that will be poverty-stricken and totally unhappy. Much as this could come about, there is such a thing as free will. The person will have to focus and orient their endeavours to benefit themselves, rather than only for other people at the expense of themselves. It is very rare to see absolutely nothing at all for the Sun Line on the palm. Even the merest fine Line gives hope for future development. Sometimes inherited wealth or a religious vocation will show a diminished Sun Line and possibly Fate Line as well; mainly because they don't need them.

The Timing of Events

To get an idea of where we are age-wise on the Sun Line, start at the point nearest the wrist and work up the Line towards the end of it, which is nearest the third finger. The age span will be from one to seventy-plus years. The middle of the Line will represent about forty years. The Line cannot be gauged by where it crosses over the Head and Heart Lines, as they vary considerably in position.

The Starting Positions of the Sun Line

The Sun Line Starting on the Mount of the Moon
When the Sun Line starts on the Mount of the Moon, which is to the far side of the hand, it is indeed fortunate. It is seen in the hands of celebrities who rise to fame through influential friends and contacts. Those whose Line starts here and who are not working in the entertainment

business, should realize they have the ability to work with crowds, i.e. PR work, salesperson, and all areas that involve making contact with the general public.

The Sun Line Starting from the Head Line
When the Line runs from the Head Line, having been absent or sketchy before, it indicates a happy ending – because the person has at last engaged their brains! The person's latent talents and skills will be rewarded in the latter part of their lives. Their ship will have come in at last.

The Sun Line Starting from the Heart Line
Although the person has a considerable interest in the arts, they usually want to strive for success in this area. As it can lead to work that doesn't bring in much financial gain, material success may not arrive until old age.

The Sun Line Starting from the Fate Line
This shows a lot of talent regarding the arts, painting, etc, but they can expect late recognition for their work. It indicates a bright mind that strives for satisfaction, but they will only do what pleases them.

The Sun Line Starting from the Life Line
When it starts attached to the Life Line on both hands, it means they can't miss in life! They'll get considerable help along the way from all directions.

The Sun Line Starting Inside the Life Line
If it starts on the soft pad underneath the thumb (known as the Mount of Venus), they are very emotional and get their inspiration from their creative skills, and from their extreme sensitivity, even bordering on the intuitive or psychic.

The Sun Line in a Hollow Palm

This must be mentioned, as sometimes a good Sun Line runs strong, straight and true and yet the person still doesn't seem to be successful and contented. If this is so then look to the centre of the palm and if you find that it seems to be sunk in the middle like a bowl, then this will be the reason for the ill luck. The sunken centre comes from being discouraged as a child, or even unwanted. To overcome this problem the person can work on improving their self worth and image.

The Ending Positions of the Sun Line

The Sun Line Ending on the Jupiter Mount

When this Line ends on the Mount of Jupiter, it usually indicates distinction through attainment of power. There is tremendous determination and they are born to climb high, because of their ambition and energy.

The Sun Line Ending on the Saturn Mount

The Line may branch off and end on the Mount of Saturn, located under the third finger. This gives the wisdom that the Saturn Finger, the second finger, possesses.

The Sun Line Ending on the Apollo Mount

When the Line ends here under the third finger, it shows that the person has seen their talents through to the end. If a star marking appears on it, it denotes brilliant success. A double star is rarely seen, but when it appears dazzling fame will result. A star appearing anywhere lower down the Line will show the age at which success is achieved.

The Sun Line Ending on the Mercury Mount

If the Sun Line ends on this mount under the fourth finger of Mercury, then shrewdness will be added to its other qualities. The result will not only be wealth, but a high reputation.

The Depth and Furrowing of the Sun Line

Shallow When the depth of the Line is shallow and appears thin, it unfortunately weakens the Line. The person never grasps the goodies from life; they appear hard done by. This is mainly because no one told them they can have it in the first place. The underlings

Deep If this Line is of medium depth then it shows there is a good chance of achieving personal success. Over-deep, and the person seems artificial; you never know who they really are because they exaggerate. Deception creeps in; the con man.

Width When this Line is spread out and appears very broad, the person is inclined towards overindulgence. They can spend money recklessly – drinking champagne when they only have beer money. They are rather inclined to bad taste.

The Wavy Sun Line

The person will, through lack of concentrative power, sabotage their own success. An artistic career will be hindered because of the lack of commitment. The jack-of-all-trades and master of none.

Colour

The Sun Line wears the Gold Badge of Success.

Pink If the Line has a lovely rosy-pink hue, the person will have a sunny nature with a life full of promise for as long as the Line appears.

Pale When the Line appears pale, almost white, it shows that although there is artistic ability the person will not have the physical or mental energy to carry it through.

Yellow Yellow is a very good colour to show up in this Line. It indicates an expansion of good fortune – the unobtainable now becomes obtainable. The person is allowed access to money and material wealth. Able to get one's needs met.

Blue Blue in the Sun Line can indicate a highly inventive nature. The person will not sell their soul for fame or monetary gains. They work with honour and sincerity. They do well in the realm of science and the arts.

Red If the Line is a lovely strong red and is also straight, then the person has exceptionally strong artistic leanings. Their life will be devoted to a creative vocation.

Dark Black-red The tendency when the Line is dark red is for the person to veer towards odd tastes in personal pleasures. Money will come through ill-gotten gains. The person could be drawn to provide entertainment for others using debased exploits.

Positive Aspects of the Sun Line
Creative aptitude. Artistic Success. Fame. Good Will. Financial Prosperity. Progress. Celebrity Status. Personal Satisfaction. Breakthrough. Self Esteem.

Negative Aspects of the Sun Line
Addiction. Debauchery. People pleaser. Blocked. Retreat. Shallow. Builds ideas on quicksand.

Transformation of the Sun Line

The essence of greatness is the ability to choose personal fulfilment in circumstances where others choose madness. (Dr Wayne W. Dyer)

- Winners get it together with their loved ones, their friends, and with the community in which they live. They also love their careers, but are not married to them. Winners vote and care about the government of their cities, states and nations, and about their effectiveness, fairness and honesty.
- Life is a celebration.
- Make eye-to-eye contact an important part of your assertive behaviour.
- Learn to feel happiness flowing joyfully through you.
- Keep your sunny side up – live, laugh, love, and be happy.
- Treat your stress responses with the same respect you treat any other habit.
- Look for the silver lining.
- Change your mind if you want to.
- Let go of the critic within, and loosen up.
- Choose an effective, fulfilling life.
- Success smells sweet – treat yourself to floral after-shave/perfume.
- Set your boundaries and don't let anyone move them unless it suits you.
- Spend ten minutes each day as your 'ideas' slot.
- Increase your vacation time and time away from work.
- You have the right to offer no reason or excuses to justify your behaviour.

- What one loses, one loses – make no mistake about that – so develop an appreciation for the present moment.
- If nature wins, everyone wins. Eat organic today.
- Live all you can. It's a mistake not to.
- Look behind the self for the meaning of life.
- Each day is precious. Live it as if it were your last.
- Learn from the past and build for the future.
- Become the total person, visionary and humanist.
- Practise the win-win attitude – when I help *you* to win, then *I* win.

Healing Meditation

A commitment to yourself is made on a level deeper than the mind. Conceive of a possibility so extraordinary that simply embarking on its realization transforms your life.

Close your eyes and visualize the top of your head opening and a beautiful golden light beaming straight down into your body. Let this rich golden ray move around your diaphragm and under your ribs, penetrating your stomach, so that it enhances your willpower, giving you a greater sense of the self. Allow this gold to flood the rest of your body, giving your confidence a boost. Take a deep breath and exhale. Do this three times, and then RELAX.

FOURTEEN

THE MERCURY
Line

> *Only do always in health what you have often*
> *promised to do when you are sick.*
>
> ANONYMOUS

The Mercury Line is known as the Health Line. It lies on the outer side of the palm underneath the fourth finger. During the development of palmistry this Line acquired many names such as the Milky Way. In the Middle Ages it was called the Hepatic or Liver Line because it was believed to have an attachment to the person's liver. The Mercury Line is still known today in modern palmistry as the Line of Health. This Line's name and characteristics come from the fourth finger, named after the god Mercury, the messenger. The mercurial character has the gift of words, is a great PR person, has a bright, sparkling personality and keen, swift movements. In referring to this Line, the palmist in ancient times knew that geniality only comes about if we are not liverish. If we are affected in that area all joy seems to leave us. It is said that the absence of this Line is to be desired, as without it the dreaded biliousness and nausea that is associated with liverish, poor digestion doesn't occur. The advantage of a missing Mercury Line is that perfect digestion and functioning of the stomach contributes greatly to the clear head and abounding energy that are essential qualities for business dealings.

When the Line is present then it is most desirable if it is straight and clear with no breaks. The perfect Mercury Line is one that originates from the mount of Neptune. This is the place near the wrist, positioned between the third and fourth fingers. It runs in a straight line ending underneath the little finger. When the line is medium-deep and only has the palest of colour it indicates a good combination of both health and the practical side of life. Nearly everyone has this Line in some form or other even if it is only a little fine line etched here and there. It is rare to see a palm without any indications of the Mercury Line at all.

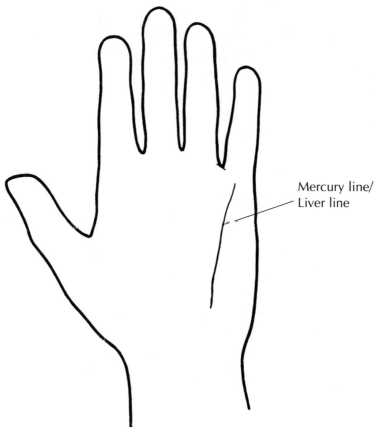

Mercury line/
Liver line

Figure 18: The Mercury Line

What to Look For

The Line runs from the base of the hand near the wrist straight up the palm to just under the fourth finger. If the Line is long and straight with no breaks present then compare it with the Life Line which, if it appears a little weak, will be boosted by the strong Mercury Line to support longevity. If there are breaks in a straight, strong line then they represent extra concern with health.

When the Line is present in one hand only, then notice whether it's on the hand of the past or the hand of the present and future. Whichever it is, extra care must be given to strengthen the person's constitution. When the Mercury Line consists of several smaller, feathery lines with breaks in between, each line will indicate several different health problems or the same problem that keeps recurring. The gaps in the Line show an absence from ill health at those times.

As much as you can evaluate the person's health with the Mercury Line, it also gives an indication of the subject's ability to be able to express themselves and execute their talents to the best advantage, if their well-being physically allows them to. The Mercury Line monitors the subject's performance in all sections. If you are healthy then you are able to carry through whatever is embarked upon.

Dividing the Mercury Line into Three Sections

The Starting Section – Birth to 25 Years
The start of the Mercury Line begins at the lower end of the palm and goes up toward the fourth, the 'baby' finger.

If there is a Line at this early period it could show poor health as a child. Sometimes the Line is only present from birth to young adulthood. It can weaken, and disappear from the middle and end part of the palm. When this happens it shows the person has overcome their earlier delicate health problems. If there is a square box on the Line it is good as it is sign of repair.

The Middle Section – 25 to 50 Years
If the Line is still there, and continues from the start, then the person has not improved health-wise from childhood. When the Line starts in this mid-section the person is likely to develop health problems

during the 25–50 years period. Many criss-cross lines running over the Line at the mid-section shows that worrying helps to keep the health impaired.

If this section appears on both hands of a child, it allows something to be done that will help the Line to disappear, which it will if the cause of the health problem is removed.

The End Section – 50 to 70 Years

If the Line is present in this age bracket, it is best that it is a good, clean, and not too-deep line with no adverse markings. But, it is less likely to be seen as the person ages. You may find that this latter section has many islands or chaining on it if present. This usually indicates that the person has been a heavy smoker and is now in possession of a pair of not too-healthy lungs.

Extra care of health needs to be taken from 40 years on. When the latter part of the Mercury Line starts from the Head Line, even if the health is reasonable, it will still show that great stress is present.

The Timing of Events

The timing of this line can be gauged by starting at the wrist end of the Line, following the Line up to the palm, ending underneath the small Finger of Mercury. The age starts from nought to 70 years plus. Do not forget that the absence of this Line on the hand shows perfect health.

The Starting Positions for the Mercury Line

The Mercury Line Starting from the Mount of the Moon

This is a straight line starting from the Mount and running from the wrist up to under the fourth finger. It's placed on the opposite side of the palm from the thumb. This can show a person who is very insightful as it is close to the Line of Intuition (see Chapter 15) if it is present in the hand.

The Mercury Line Starting from the Line Life

It is always best that the Mercury Line does not touch the Life Line, because although the Mercury Line beginning from the Life Line shows a very articulate, lively personality, they will have a tendency to hypochondria. Extreme cases become paranoid about germs and personal hygiene. It can sometimes indicate a weakness of heart, but not always heart disease.

The Mercury Line Starting from the Mount of Venus

When the Line starts from below the thumb by the Mount of Venus and runs in a straight line to below the fourth finger on the Mercury Mount, it implies a probable weakness in the digestive area. The family may demand a lot from a person with this line placement, who could be made ill by trying to fulfil family obligations.

The Ending Positions for the Mercury Line

The Mercury Line Ending on the Mercury Mount

It is best not to have this line showing at all as it approaches the Mount of Mercury. Its absence would denote perfect health and general well being later on. If it is present this Line usually appears weaker because of the person's ageing. Any little lines branching off upwards to the Mercury finger are a good sign indicating added help with health matters towards the end of life. Small lines pointing downwards show health concerns. Extra care is needed to keep well and fit.

The Mercury Line Ending on the Apollo Mount
It is rare to see a Mercury Line veering over the palm towards the Apollo Mount. When this does happen it means that the person has gained enough success which financially has enabled them to acquire any medical help they may need in later life.

The Absent Mercury Line Myth
The myth of the Mercury Line is that it is best not to have one at all, and that perfect health comes from the complete absence of it showing up on the palm. However, if it does show up in some form or other, it is best to understand that care will have to be taken concerning the physical constitution. At least with this Line's appearance it will make the subject actively aware of health matters.

Depth and Furrowing of the Mercury Line
Shallow A shallow Line is a blessing as far as the owners' health is concerned. It means an absence of illness and generally a good constitution. Can possess a stiff personality.

Deep The deeper this line is the more impaired the digestion can be, particularly in old age. Generally poorer health as the person matures. Must watch out for any tendency towards brain conditions.

Width A broad Line in the early part of a child's life could mean a lot of fevers when young, when it is hard to get any resistance to infections due to a low immune system. As an adult the person would be wiser to keep a check on their health generally, and not to take liberties. If this broadness appears later on, it can show that the adult is rather inclined to talk too much for their own good.

Wavy Mercury Line

Unfortunately, a weaving Mercury Line can indicate biliousness, and if the hand is cold and clammy it will be of the worst kind. Not too good in business either. Can show a tendency towards a weak heart. Watch out for bad teeth.

Colour

The Mercury Line wears the White Badge of the Healer.

The colour seen on the Mercury line will represent tendencies to certain ailments and give indications of ill health. (Always check with a doctor if in doubt.)

Pink Pink suggests that the person is never seriously ill, but never really well either.

Pale The paler this Line or fragments of the Line, the better the health will be.

White White indicates a leaning towards certain minor ailments, but if they do occur they will be of little consequence and soon over-come.

Yellow This is not a good colour to have on the Mercury line. It most definitely signifies that there could be problems in the liver and digestive area. Check diet, lifestyle and don't drink alcohol.

Blue Could indicate migraine and sinus problems. Circulation may be sluggish, so take more exercise. The person will need to look after themselves a bit, and not take chances with their health. The heart and chest are the areas to watch. In other words, with a cold, go to bed.

Red Prone to headaches and possibly blood pressure and rheumatism. Disorders of the blood could indicate the person bottles up emotions and then explodes into temper, which is not good for the nerves.

Dark Red Poor circulation. A disposition towards alcoholism.

Positive Mercury Aspects
Alive. Content. Perfect Health. Security. Radiant. Communicator. Articulate. Good ideas.

Negative Mercury Aspects
Martyrdom. Impatience. Restriction. Vacillation. Slippery. Cynic.

Transformation of the Mercury Line

Change cannot be avoided. Change provides the opportunity for innovation. It gives you the chance to demonstrate your creativity.

- Forget the words should or shouldn't.
- Take charge of yourself.
- Travel as far as you can go.
- Communication is the name of the game.
- Feel the fear and do it anyway.
- The word is mightier than the sword.
- Improve the quality of your voice – take elocution lessons.
- Learn correct breathing.

- Make sure that anything you start you carry through to the end.
- Learn to be an active listener – keep quiet.
- Become involved in outside activities and organizations.
- Learn stress management so as to improve the immune system and decrease illness.
- Curiosity is the doorway that stimulates growth, joy and health.
- Don't carry unnecessary burdens.
- Practise the white light healing meditation three times a day.
- Let the real you stand up.
- One cannot heal fragmentation by walking through fragmentation.
- Let's move out of the history of ill health and move into the now of wellness.
- Remember the light of the self transforms the darkness of illness.
- At any moment you, who are God, can move mountains.
- Every day, and in every way I'm getting stronger and *stronger*.

Healing Meditation

Let yourself out of the prison of ill health. Reclaim the magic of the small child. Fatigue will disappear. Joy will return. Allow your heart to open just a little bit each day. Illness will vanish and decrease. You will be well.

Close your eyes and visualize the top of your head opening and a beautiful pure white light bearing straight down into your body. As you take each breath into you, pull this brilliant white light into your lungs and exhale the darkness from your system on the outgoing breath. Allow this light to detox and cleanse the body. RELAX.

Minor Lines Connected to the Mercury Line

Social Marking – Medical Stigmata

There may be several short, fine lines on the Mount of Mercury that start at the bottom of the Mercury Finger and connect at the end of their run near the Mercury Line. They are also known as the medical stigmata. To possess these lines shows the person would make a good counsellor or even a psychiatrist. There is a flare for socializing and the extra gift of being able to influence people by the voice, whatever the chosen field.

FIFTEEN

THE MINOR
Lines

These lines may or may not be present on the palm but are worth knowing if they are.

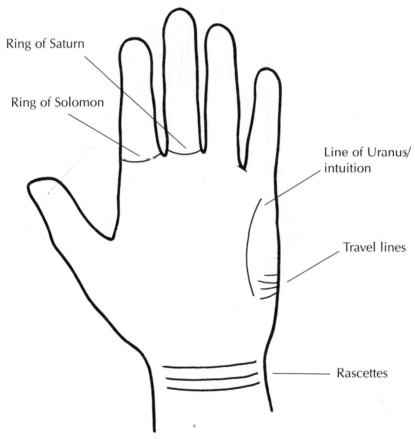

Ring of Saturn

Ring of Solomon

Line of Uranus/ intuition

Travel lines

Rascettes

Figure 19: The Minor Lines

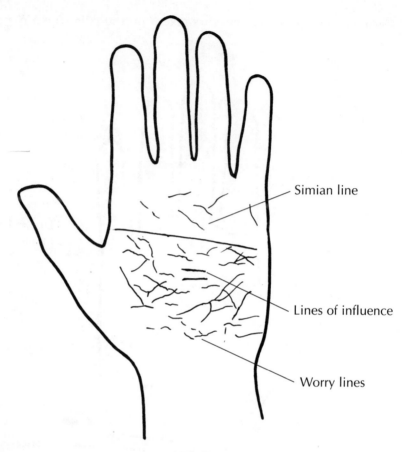

Figure 20: Other Minor Lines

The Rascettes

The rascettes or, as they are commonly called, the bracelets, form circles of lines just below the palm on the wrist. There are usually three distinct bands but sometimes there are four or more. I feel each one of them represents thirty years of good luck, health and happiness. The one furthest away from the bottom of the palm is the recorder for the first 30 years of a person's life. The second one indicates the middle years and the bracelet nearest the palm shows the latter 30 years of life. It is interesting to compare the differences between them. You may find the first rascette line, the one furthest from the palm, to be very thin and broken which indicates a poor start in life resulting in struggle later on. The second one may appear stronger because the person has been able to pull themselves through. The third one could be the best of the lot, which means that they are a late developer and have the best yet to come.

If the last bracelet has a curve in the middle which creeps onto the palm, look out for gynaecological and urinological problems after 50 years of age. Being aware of this up front means that you can take measures to prevent it, such as exercise and diet, etc. The Rascettes can have breaks in them, which means a change of direction in life, or they can be chained, indicating problems along the way. Any fine line rising from the rascettes lines gives an indication of extra travelling. It is fortunate to have all three rascettes/bracelets strong and clear, proving that the person has had an easy run in life.

A minor or incomplete rascette line indicates something started or coming into one's life, but ending quickly or not followed through.

The Line of Intuition

This is also known as the Uranus Line and appears as a semi-circle that starts on the Lunar Mount and circles around towards the centre of the palm and ends up on the mount of Mercury. It indicates an uncanny insight regarding intuitive matters. The possessors of this half-moon looking Line are extremely sensitive, with a bright lively mind. They love anything connected to the psychic arts. If the Line is broken it is best to leave psychic matters alone as the health could be damaged, particularly the nervous system, if the mystic arts are attempted.

Travel Lines

The major area to look for travel indications is at the side of the palm. The Lines start from the end of the Head Line and travel low down on the palm's edge, towards the wrist, starting around from the percussion side of the hand, and end on the Lunar Mount. The longer they are the more time spent travelling. If the Line turns slightly upwards it will be a successful trip. Turning downwards could show disappointment.

Moving House

The Lines that indicate a change of address or living quarters are seen as lines that come around onto the palm from the percussion area and end on the Lunar Mount. They are contained in the space between the Head and Heart Line. Each Line will represent a house move. The longer the Line the longer the stay in the property.

The Line of Neptune – Via Lasciva

The Via Lasciva Line runs from the bottom of the Life Line and moves across the palm, ending on the lower part of the Lunar Mount. It is a rare Line and shows the person has a tendency towards addiction. They have to be careful that alcohol and drugs do not overwhelm them. It also gives indication of allergic reactions to substances. Can be overcome by their emotions and sexual desires.

Lines of Influence

Support Lines

Any Line that travels alongside a major line is known as a sister line to the line it follows. It gives support and added strength to the section it covers.

Influence Lines

These are the little lines that can be seen anywhere on the palm that are running horizontally across it. They indicate the intervention of other people – it can either be good or bad but it allows the person to become wiser through experience.

Worry Lines

When there are many fine lines crossing the palm in all directions, it indicates the worrier; a highly sensitive person who always seems to be at the effect of other people's causes. These lines are always found on soft, fine skin.

Ring of Solomon

This Line can connect to the Heart Line but usually it curves around the base of the Jupiter finger. It is a rare Line and is seen more often on female palms. It indicates psychic power connected to the mystic arts, plus keen intelligence. On a male hand it shows extreme sensitivity. The Ring is connected to wisdom with the ability to teach. Drawn to philosophical studies.

The Simian Line

The Simian Line is a rare Line that appears when the Heart and the Head Lines are joined together, showing itself as one straight Line across the palm. The person possessing this Line has an intensity in their emotions, going from one extreme to the other. Often at odds with the world and their fellow men, as they are unpredictable. They are usually very clever intellectually, but unable to combine their love-life with a career. Yet they are able to accomplish anything they put their minds to because of their strong concentrative powers. It is very rare for the Line to appear on both hands, but where it does, it can indicate genius.

WAY *of*

Ring of Saturn

The Ring of Saturn is a small circle that runs around the base of the second/middle finger. This sign acts as a warning. It indicates changes, but because it lays across the Saturn Mount the active energy flow from the finger above and the Saturn Line below it are hindered. When strong and unbroken, it is unwise for the person to take chances, as danger is lurking. Risky pursuits are not for them.

If the circle is broken and faint, the less inhibiting it will be. Fortunately the sign is a rare one, and as it in not a particularly positive one, is luckily not often seen.

Markings

The markings on the palm have a very special place in palmistry. A mark can change the meaning of any section of the palm for good or for ill. Whenever you come across a mark of any kind check in this section to get an accurate understanding of its meaning. Marks record the past, present and future so always be careful and aware of the place that it appears, as this will tell you when it is likely to occur or whether it's already happened.

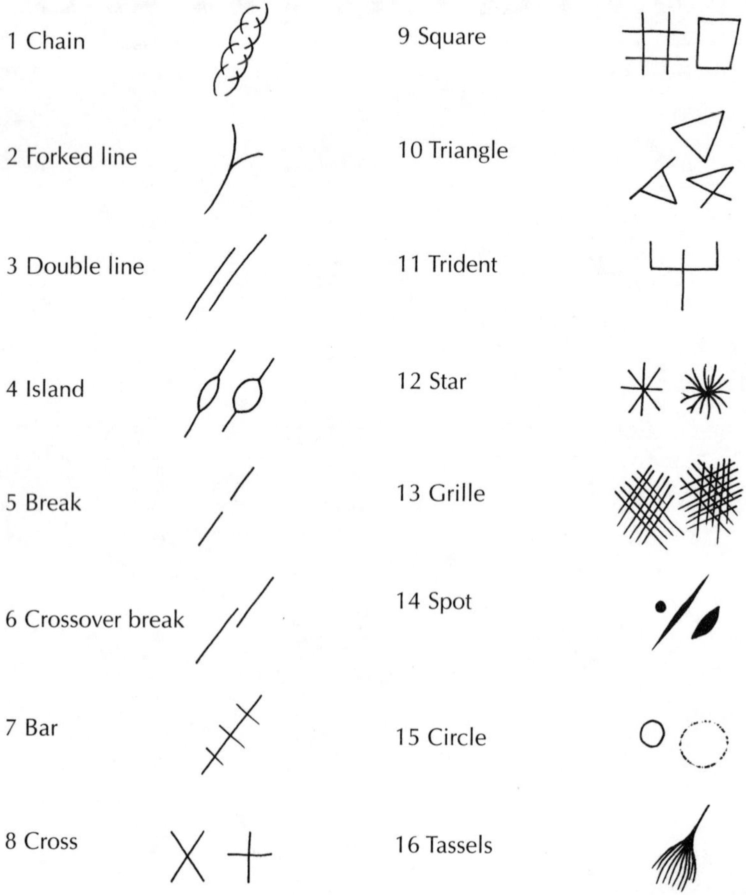

1 Chain

2 Forked line

3 Double line

4 Island

5 Break

6 Crossover break

7 Bar

8 Cross

9 Square

10 Triangle

11 Trident

12 Star

13 Grille

14 Spot

15 Circle

16 Tassels

Figure 21: Markings

1 Chain

When chaining appears anywhere on a line it weakens that particular part. The longer it continues the longer that period of time for bad luck. Indecision.

2 Forked Line

The fork indicates there are two paths to take. A division of interest. A tendency to contradict oneself.

3 Double Line

If a Line has another Line next to it following it along, it creates a reinforcing and strengthening protection.

4 Island

An island always shows some problems in the functioning of the person's life until the island ends. Stress period.

5 Break

Indicates unpleasant interruptions. A clean break indicates something ending. Look to health problems.

6 Crossover Break

Not so serious as the clean break. Although a difficult period it does eventually work out for the best.

7 Bar

An unpleasant experience has left its mark. Times of opposition and barriers.

8 Cross

Signifies a shock or upheaval at that time, unless it is found between the Head and Heart Lines, indicating psychic ability.

9 Square

A good sign to have anywhere on the palm as it gives protection. The positive overcoming the negative.

10 Triangle

Represents harmony peace and good fortune. Spiritual learning can increase at the time it appears. Intellectual and creative talent combined.

11 Trident

An extremely fortunate sign to have on the palm as it brings success threefold. Health wealth and happiness.

12 Star

Sudden happenings, triumphant or tragic. Depends where it is placed. Best place is at the end of the Sun Line. Anywhere else be cautious as it can go either way. Lots of stars denotes an interesting life.

13 Grille

Dissipates energy. Confusion and uncertainty at these times. Generally dissipates progress.

14 Spot

A spot or dot always calls a halt, a temporary stop. A string of dots close together shows a lot of obstacles to overcome.

15 Circle

A rare sign to see. Good if seen on the end of the Sun Line on the Mount of Apollo. A warning if found anywhere else.

16 Tassels

Time of break down. When this sign appears on a person's palm they must sit down and work out what to do.

Rare Markings

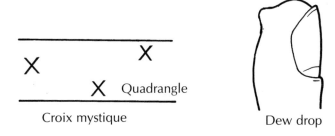

Figure 22: Rare Markings

The Croix Mystique
This marking, when present, is found only in the area called the Quadrangle which is the space between the Head and Heart Lines (Chapter 18). It is more commonly called The Mystic Cross. When this Cross falls beneath the Finger of Saturn, the third finger, and is equally balanced in its crossed lines, it indicates a talent for psychic and spiritual work. If the Cross is badly formed, it's best to leave the mystic arts alone, as the person will become engrossed with superstition.

A Cross that is small or placed in other areas of the Quadrangle, indicates that the person has supernatural talents, but is not yet ready to use them.

The Dew Drop
This can, at times, be more a protuberance than a mark. It is a little mound of flesh similar to a droplet, that appears on the finger tips – hence the name Dew Drop. It is quite a rare marking, but when present it indicates a talent for 'hands on' healing. The more finger tips it appears on, the stronger the ability.

183

SEVENTEEN

THE

Mounts

The raised and rounded mounds of flesh on the palm are called *mounts*. They can be regarded as landmarks. Any line that passes, touches or ends on one of these will take on some of the characteristics associated with that mount. There are basically eight of them although some palmists differ in opinion regarding the number. I have found that it helps to establish a greater understanding of these pads if eight are studied.

Four of them appear as little raised pads at the base of the fingers, and they take on the name of the finger directly above them. The other four are placed on the outer part of the palm, two each side. They take the names of Greek Gods and the characteristics associated with that God will be present in the personality aspect of the mount. It was believed that vital fluids collect in these pads, where a multitude of nerve endings gave them the life-force energy. They become reservoirs of strength and the power of each mount is related to its size. The bigger it is the more pronounced the qualities of its name. It is important to compare the mount on each hand. They may differ considerably from one hand to the other. Although each hand will have all the mount positions, it is more fortunate to have the most balanced mounts on the Hand of the Future.

What to Look For

When scanning the mounts it is best to look at the basic hand first. If it is thick and chubby then the mounts will be more pronounced than on the slim hand. Look at the hand for any raised lumps and bumps. Mounts come in three sizes: large, medium and small. The large can become overlarge when negative traits predominate, and the small mount can become a hollow when most qualities of that mount are wanting. Also take into account the mounts at the outer parts of the palm. They give a general guide to the size of a normal mount for that particular palm.

185

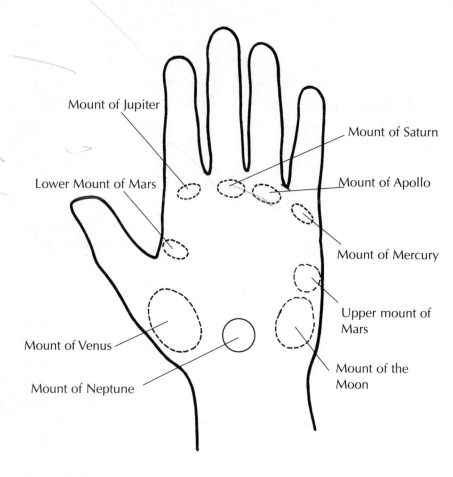

Mount of Jupiter

Mount of Saturn

Lower Mount of Mars

Mount of Apollo

Mount of Mercury

Mount of Venus

Upper mount of Mars

Mount of Neptune

Mount of the Moon

Figure 23: The Mounts

When you start looking for the mounts this is best done by using a magnifying glass. You may notice at the apex of the mount, three ridges of skin coming together, causing a slight tip to appear in the middle of the mount just the same as the top of a mountain. This apex is a perfect guide as to whether a mount is misplaced or not. If the apex is directly under the middle of the base of the finger it is attached to then the qualities of the mount will be accessed to the full. If it is not directly beneath and falls somewhere between two fingers, then it starts to take on some of the underlying characteristics of the adjoining finger as well. The effects will not be as strong as if it were directly under just one finger. Rarely, all or almost all of the mounts will fall between the fingers.

When examining the mounts check to see which is the most prominent. This will be the dominant mount and the qualities of that mount will be the leader of all others.

The length and shape of the mount's finger must also be taken into account. If the finger above it is short and slim, the characteristics of the mount will be less than if the finger is long and thick.

The Consistency of a Mount

All mounts vary in their consistency. Some are very soft to the touch, and others are extremely hard.

The Perfect Mount
When pressed, the perfect mount should respond with a springiness, and quickly return to its original shape. This indicates a balance of all the attributes belonging to the mount.

The Soft Mount
A soft and flabby mount means the energy of the mount dissipates quickly, weakening its effects. The possessor of a soft mount is inclined to be a dreamer and a sensual romantic.

The Hard Mount
A hard mount belongs to the dogmatic plodder. Principled, and rigid in thought and deed, they can appear to be unlovable.

The Height of the Mount

The Perfect Mount

The most desired mount of all is the medium mount. When all the mounts appear on the hand as medium with no displacements or adverse marks, then it is indeed considered most fortunate. The person with perfect mounts will have an added bonus of good-will that can only enhance the rest of the hand.

The Medium-Height Mount

The medium-shaped mount is round and in proportion to the constitution of the hand, revealing that the person will, according to the identity of the pad, be well balanced and able to cope with the characteristics that are implied. The qualities are at their best. It is the most desired mount to have.

The High Mount

When the mount goes beyond medium to a higher mound then it is termed a strong mount. The qualities attached will be well to the fore. The person's nature will be strong and they will have vitality and zest for life.

The Overly-Large Mount

If the mount is abnormally prominent then too much force will accompany the implications of that mount. Impatience and self-indulgence are quite common. The character is often overly dominant.

The Flat Mount

A mount is flat when it is indistinguishable from the rest of the palm. In running the finger across a flat mount it seems smooth, without any rise in flesh at all. There is no protection for the nerve endings or the blood cells in that area and the qualities of the mount will be lacking in the person's character.

The Hollow Mount

Sometimes an actual indentation appears in the place where a mount should be, almost as if a scoop of flesh has been hollowed out. This indicates ineffectuality and a poor physical constitution. As health improves, the mount can miraculously fatten up and start to rise.

The Bumpy Mount

A mount can appear uneven with lumps and bumps rather than a nice round, smooth hill. If it is so then the meanings of that mount will be unable to get a stronghold. The energy of the mount will get started only to be cut short again. The more bumps there are the more disruption will occur, which in turn weakens the mount.

The Absent Mount Myth

It is suggested that a flat or hollow mount symbolizes no advantage whatsoever – only a total lack of benefit from the 'missing' mount. Even a depleted mount can be considered as present and active, although its power is somewhat weakened. Look for any fine lines that may cross the skin where the mount should be. If any vertical lines run down the mount, then these are a good sign and represent a link to the positive signs of the particular mount. If there are lines running horizontally across these lines, then they conceal the positive aspects and shift the emphasis of the non-existent pad into the negative traits of the mount. Look to the negative traits that are given in the corresponding Lines chapter for extra information.

The Position and Meanings of the Eight Mounts

The Mount of Jupiter

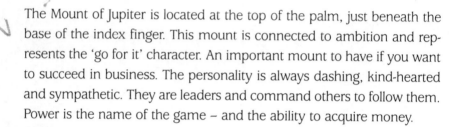

Every blade of grass has its Angel that bends over it and whispers, Grow, Grow ...

THE TALMUD

The Mount of Jupiter is located at the top of the palm, just beneath the base of the index finger. This mount is connected to ambition and represents the 'go for it' character. An important mount to have if you want to succeed in business. The personality is always dashing, kind-hearted and sympathetic. They are leaders and command others to follow them. Power is the name of the game – and the ability to acquire money.

Medium-Height Mount

When the Mount is medium in size, a good, strong, forthright character is present. They will have zest, energy and drive because they are extremely ambitious. A lover of rituals. Self-confident and generous, they command respect.

High Mount

When the Mount is high then the working life comes before everything else. A believer in peace, not war, but adheres to law and order only when they make the rules. A larger-than-life character. Requires honesty from people so becomes a pursuer of the fraudulent.

Overly-Large Mount

Arrogant and overbearing. Marries for position and money rather than love. Has sacrificed the heart for the head. Can be the ruthless bully. Must win at any price.

Flat Mount

Inclined to selfishness and can be lazy. Never seem to get any projects off the ground. Can be inconsiderate because they don't think very deeply. Lacks confidence.

The Mount of Saturn

 The secret of happiness is not in doing what one likes but in liking what one has to do.

JAMES BARRIE

The Mount of Saturn is located at the top of the palm, just beneath the base of the second finger. The Saturn character is seen as a hard worker who is cautious and prudent, a reliable person with a strong sense of duty. Marriage is sacred to them. This mount has a strong other side to it. Either the person is remarkably successful and very independent, kindly and devoted to the service of humanity or they are despondent and hard-natured to the point of unkindness. There is a dimension of Saturn that likes solitude, hence marriage is viewed cautiously. The Saturn nature can become obsessed with doom and gloom.

Medium-Height Mount

It is best if this mount is medium to slight as it then weakens the gloomy outlook that is part of the Saturn temperament. Saturn represents patience and caring, is very studious, and is able to take responsibility. Fidelity and self-awareness are also positive traits. A medium mount is able to moderate Saturn's need for aloneness, giving them the ability to share.

High Mount

The possessor of this mount can be too analytic and cynical, and can be quite bigoted, but will still have a great desire for knowledge. Care must be taken not to withdraw from life and become reclusive. Attracted to medicine and science.

Overly-Large Mount

It is unusual to see an over-large Saturn mount; responsibility is taken too seriously because of fear. Ruled by ulterior motives. The pessimist. Coerces others into the wrong direction for personal gain.

Flat Mount

If the Saturn mount is flat then the person can be hard to get along with. Depression can set in and the person will be hard put to see the good in anything. The flatter it is the weaker the will. Miserliness is another trait. Displays a frivolous outlook on life – unreliable.

The Mount of the Apollo

> *Are you willing to create the possibility of unlimited possibilities?*
>
> SELF TRANSFORMATION CENTRE

The Mount of the Apollo is located at the top of the palm, just beneath the base of the third finger. This mount, also known as the Mount of the Sun, indicates a happy and genial disposition. The darker aspects of survival are kept in the background. Always looks to the brighter side of life. Extremely artistic and usually able to combine it with personal financial success. Does not harbour grievances. The sunny Apollo nature strives for success, fulfilment and happiness for everyone.

Medium-Height Mount

A medium-sized Sun mount has a good balance between the heart and the head making for a pleasant, sunny nature. Harmony can be found in the work-place and at home. Has a love of beauty that can bring in good fortune – the possessor of a lucky streak.

High Mount

On the whole the larger this mount is the stronger the desire for fame and fortune. There will be an extremely strong interest in music and the arts. Can be a little pretentious and a shade extravagant. Inclined to spend money on beautiful things that they cannot afford. Apart from this, it is one of the most desirable large mount to have.

Overly-Large Mount

As excessive interest in the love of pleasure. Will go to any lengths to have a good time, even at the expense of safety. Creative talents are scattered. Vain.

Flat Mount

Totally cut off from the emotions. Untouched by any sense of feeling. Can be aimless and dull, and has no interest in the arts whatsoever. Rather inclined to do things at the expense of themselves.

The Mount of Mercury

> *The words that enlighten the soul are more*
> *precious than jewels.*
>
> Mazrat Inayal Khan

The Mount of the Mercury is located at the top of the palm, beneath the fourth finger. As Mercury is the messenger then this mount emphasizes the ability to communicate, and possesses great powers of expression, particularly through the voice. The personality is lively and persuasive and needs company and variety. A hard worker, quite often found in promotional work and the media. This mount relates more to the brain than anything else, yielding a quick-thinking agility of mind, wittiness, and adaptability. They are vivacious, keen and shrewd. Mercury loves married life but can be envious if the partner has more success than they. Extremely active both mentally and physically, with many varied capabilities.

Medium-Height Mount

When this mount is of medium size it aids the rest of the hand's aspects to communicate more fully. Mercuries are incredible fun to be with when on form. They have unusual personalities as they fly where others fear to tread. Can charm the birds out of the trees with their sweet talk. Points to commercial talent. Usually good at mathematics.

High Mount

Incredible sense of humour but check that there is a person underneath the jokes. In all business endeavours they are in a class of their own where a keen subtle manner is required. Watch out for glibness and outsmarting themselves.

Overly-Large Mount

Thinks only of the self first. The con man lurks within. Will use the gift of the gab to cheat. The light-fingered thief comes to the fore if they are tempted. Must watch out for dishonest practices. Conceit gets in the way of intimacy.

Flat Mount

Uncertainty creeps in. Constantly changing their lives for fear of consistency. Unreliable. They can be become dull and humourless. Convinced they are a failure. Gullible.

The Mount of the Moon

> *Shoot for the moon. Even if you miss it you will*
> *land amongst the stars.*
>
> LES BROWN

The Mount of the Moon is the fleshy pad that starts by the wrist and goes half-way up the palm towards the little finger. The Mount of the Moon represents our sensitivity and imagination. It reveals our perceptiveness connecting us to our subconscious. It is the seat of our emotions that affects our moods according to the moon. The person can also be attracted to the sea. The Mount of the Moon reflects our romantic nature. When the Mount is pronounced there will be an interest in mysticism. Very intuitive. This mount gives a wide range of circumstances from genius to insanity. It is prominent in writers of romantic fiction, musicians, those in highly creative pursuits.

To judge this mount for size, hold the palm flat and look to the side of the palm to see if it curves outwards. If it does it indicates a well-formed medium size Mount of the Moon. Then look to see if there is a pad on top of the palm as well. If so, then the two pads together are considered a large lunar mount. When the outside of the palm is flat and there is not a pad on the palm it will be a low mount.

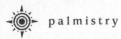

Medium-Height Mount

A medium-sized mount indicates someone with an imaginative mind able to bring their inspirations into everyday living. Shows a very romantic nature and a desire to perceive more than meets the eye. There will be great energy if the hand overall is flexible.

High Mount

Inclined to be a trifle over-imaginative. Fantasy becomes an indulgence leading to foolishness. Lives too much in the imagination. May find surviving in the real world quite hard to bear. Likes to take care of others. Strong interest in the mystic arts.

Overly-Large Mount

Cannot separate the truth from fantasy, which leads to telling lies, although they believe it to be the truth. The *deluded guru* syndrome. Inclined to over-excitement and can lose control emotionally. Insolent. Sometimes veering towards mental illness.

Flat Mount

Lacks imagination. Appears unapproachable, withdrawn and timid. Can be cold and unsympathetic. The bigot. A dull and meticulous person. Solely interested in material things and avoids anything spiritual.

The Mount of the Moon Travel Lines

Although the travel lines have already been mentioned, it is important to take into account the size of the Moon Mount and how it will affect them. Travel lines can be seen on the side of the Mount of the Moon running from the edge of the palm going towards the middle of the palm. If the Mount is large they will be strongly drawn to travel, much more than most because there will be a restlessness present. May be drawn to sailing. If the Mount is flat with travel lines present, then the person tends to be more of an 'armchair traveller'.

The Mount of Venus

When we love we hand ourselves over to receive
from another our own triumph or tragedy.

W.H. VANSTONE, *The Statue of Waiting*

The Mount of Venus is located below the base of the thumb, forming a ball that is circled by the Life Line. The Venus mount is named after the goddess of love. It connects us to our higher self, and indicates our ability to share with another. Some palmists believe it is the most important mount of all and can enhance or diminish the others according to its size. In my experience the colour aspect of this mount gives a great deal of insight into the person's happiness and contentment with life. If it is pale to white the person will be cool as regards their love life. When red there will be an anger and a coarseness within the sexual aspect. A lovely light pink indicates a good sexual energy with a warm, loving nature. The Venus mount shows our ability to let go of our inhibitions, and our passions for love and luxury combined with sensitivity.

Medium-Height Mount
When the mount is of medium size it shows a loving, warm nature: extremely human, very sensitive and generous. Desires to please others and has a love of companionship. An attraction to beauty in every form. There is great magnetism with the power to draw the opposite sex. Good vitality.

High Mount
Loves luxury. A very bright bubbly personality. The sexual side of life will be the main concern. Great lovers of life, most generous and hospitable. When in love they are devoted to their partner.

197

Overly-Large Mount

Into sleaze. Over indulgent sexual life, and with food and drink. Likes to dominate others. The sexual bully. Leads a very unconventional love life.

Flat Mount

Prone to a cold nature. Low sexual drive. A meanness of Spirit. When flat it cancels out a lot of the positiveness of the other mounts. It lowers the joy threshold of life and shows a loveless existence.

Do not despair if you have, or see that another person has a low Venus mount. The meaning can be totally directed to a weak constitution physically which can be altered by better care; or a strong love affair can increase this mount.

The Mounts of Mars

> *Wars, conflict, it's all business. One murder*
> *makes a villain. Millions a hero. Numbers*
> *sanctify.*
>
> CHARLIE CHAPLIN

There are two Mounts of Mars situated half-way up on opposite sides of the palm. As Mars is the god of war they both are connected to courage and the will to fight. There are two kinds of fighters: one who battles openly, and one who fights covertly, unseen. These have their equivalents in the Mounts of Mars. One is called the Active Lower Mount and is more aggressive, and the other is called the Passive Upper Mount. To have these mounts present at all on the palm shows that whatever comes one's way there will always be a fighting spirit present.

The Active Lower Mount of Mars

The mount lies beneath the Mount of Jupiter under the Life Line. This is also known as the positive Mount of Mars. It can be seen as a small fleshy pad at the top of the Venus mount, particularly if the thumb is brought up to lie flat against the palm.

Medium Mount

When medium-sized it represents courage, self-control and stamina. Physically brave with a cool head in a crisis. Never afraid to take risks.

High Mount

Violent by nature. Unable to control temper and aggression. Extremely competitive by nature. Great physical strength. The Amazon.

Extra-High Mount

The person who bulldozes through everyone's feelings. Wilful, prepared to do it regardless of the cost to anyone else. The bully.

Flat Mount

Here we have the coward afraid of physical pain.

The Upper Passive Mount of Mars

This second Mount of Mars lies on the opposite side of the palm immediately above the Mount of the Moon, usually between the Head and the Heart Lines, veering towards the outside of the palm. This mount is the quieter of the two and indicates a slower reaction to provocation. Nonetheless, still waters run deep and if this mount is present at all, it's best not to take liberties when dealing with this person.

Medium Mount

Able to withstand a lot of abuse before they go into action. Great self-control. Diplomatic. Morally courageous.

High Mount

Strong resistive powers. Once the mind is made up nothing other than an earthquake will shake them. Inclined to be quarrelsome.

Extra-High Mount

Can be very dangerous. Never recognizes defeat so can stay doggedly with a project when it would be best to let go. Mentally cruel.

Flat Mount

Easily discouraged. Can be a difficult person to understand. Somehow seems to lose the battle no matter how much they try. Defensive. Only interested in self-preservation.

A Rare Mount: The Neptune Mount

There is a mount that is unusual to see called the Mount of Neptune. It is located just above the wrist next to the Lunar Mount and ends before it gets to the Life Line. This little, round mound of flesh shows an extraordinary interest and ability with herbalism, and an attraction to homeopathy and essences. It indicates someone who has access to earthly pleasures and is in tune with the universe and its elements.

Money Bumps: The Four Finger Mounts

I have found a quick and reliable way of instantly assessing if the person will make or acquire money. Just look at the Jupiter, Saturn, Apollo and Mercury mounts. If they all appear as large, round mounts of equal thickness, then there is a likelihood of money being there for that person. They will never be totally without money, as somehow it will always turn up.

EIGHTEEN

THE SPACE
Zones

Reading Between the Lines/Knowledge Plus Divination

The psychic aspect of reading the palms is, of course, still that part of palmistry that cannot be taught. A psychic hand reader may or may not know the meaning of all of the lines, shapes, markings, etc, on the hands, because they don't need to. They can do it anyway. The psychic hand-reader will use the palm as a tool, as a point of focus, to link up and 'tune in' clairvoyantly.

The scientific, as distinct from the psychic hand-reader, learns the meanings of all the features which appear on the hands. Some scientific readers are intuitive, even clairvoyant, whilst many psychic readers have taken the time to learn the techniques of scientific palmistry. It is of great benefit to combine the two – knowledge plus intuition.

The only way to develop and incorporate this psychic ability is to practise reading the open spaces that are on the hands. This section on the spaces between the lines is your introduction and guide to moving forward, to begin to gain access to that untapped talent within yourself.

Whilst specific information is given here as a guide on two sets of three areas on the palm, once having learned the meaning of the Areas, they can be used as a start to move away from the intellect. In moving into the open space on the palm, you can start to pick up information that is not basically written down. These three areas will be your entrée into the psychic area, backed up first by technique. Experiment with this. Dare to allow your intuition to take over from your intellectual knowledge. But remember: first get the knowledge!

203

The Longitudinal Zones

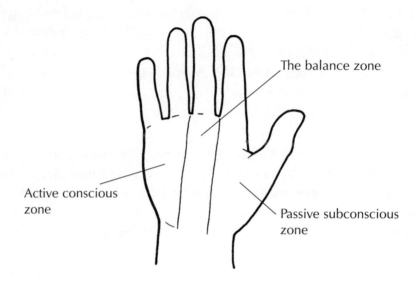

The balance zone

Active conscious
zone

Passive subconscious
zone

Figure 24: The Three Longitudinal Zones

The palm divides into three longitudinal zones. Draw an imaginary line from between the index and middle finger down to the wrist, including the thumb, and another one from between the other side of the middle finger and the third finder, including the small finger, down towards the wrist. This divides the hand into three open spaces.

First Area – Active Conscious Zone

This space which incorporated the thumb shows how we deal with the material world. If the thumb is small then there will be difficulty in this area, as the thumb shows assertion. Ambition is shown by a good strong index finger. Ego and intellectual pursuits are connected to this area.

Second Area – The Balance Zone

This space between the other two zones assists in keeping an energy balance between the two. As this space houses the Line of Saturn it can regulate both zones from one extreme to the other. It helps if the Saturn Finger is of a good medium length which further keeps things under control. It moves energy towards outward promoting endeavours such as careers and the work place so that life can be enhanced.

Third Area – The Passive Subconscious Zone

This is the space that is on the furthest part of the palm incorporating the little finger. Instinctual capacity and creative matters start in this area. If the mercury finger is short, there will be difficult speaking up for oneself, which means nothing is started or finished. Emotional and sensitive feelings are hidden here.

Latitudinal Zones

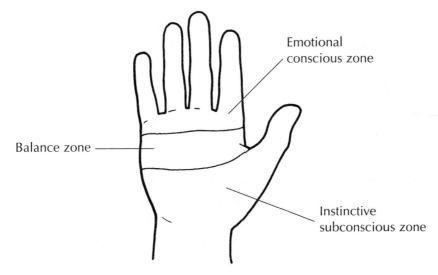

Figure 25: The Latitudinal Zones

The palm can be divided into three latitudinal areas. This is another way of exploring the palm when reading. A line is drawn from just below the Jupiter mount straight across the palm and another one down by the base of the thumb, straight over to the other side of the palm. This divides the palm into three sections.

First Area – The Emotional Conscious Zone

This space across the top of the palm is just below the finger's base. If it is well marked, the mounts in this area are well-rounded with lots of positive markings and strong ends to the major lines. This denotes an ability to connect to other people and the world outside. If this area has many positive markings, it indicates ambition, power, business acumen, artistic creativity, and the ability to grasp life's opportunities.

If this area is relatively flat and featureless, the emotional life will suffer.

Second Area – The Balance Zone

This middle zone combines both senses and reason. A strong, well-marked second area indicates a balance leading to bounty in a very concrete way. It also helps to balance the Emotional Consciousness zone by balancing out the more extreme aspects of the other two zones to promote wealth and happiness.

If this space is relatively unmarked and the palm is thin then the intellectual abilities don't bear fruit. Common sense is lacking.

Third Area – The Instinctive Subconscious Zone

The lowest zone on the palm reveals our hidden motives. Rich and full markings in this space enable our dreams to become a reality; our deepest desires couple with imagination and intuition.

Few lines in this area and flat mounts mark a mundane life.

Reading the Quadrants

Dividing the Palm into Squares

There are four quadrant sections in the palm, which are useful as they give further information regarding mental, emotional and physical aspects of the person. The use of quadrants provides another framework for the hand's information. To get the benefit of the quadrant system, you must first of all become acquainted with the lines and markings of the palm as for other readings.

Dividing the palm into four allows the palmist to rapidly get an idea of the strengths and weaknesses represented by each quadrant. If, for example, three quarters of the palm are well marked and a quarter is not, the personal aspects represented in the weak quarter can be worked on to bring the person's life up to the standards expressed in the other quarters.

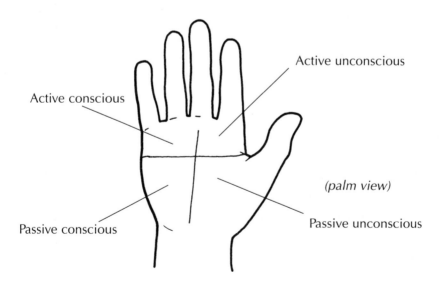

Figure 26: The Quadrants

First Area – The Active Conscious Quadrant

The Active Conscious quadrant includes the thumb and index finger, half of the middle finger, and the upper part of the hand. This outer active area is connected to social attributes and how we relate to the outside world.

Second Area – The Active Unconscious Quadrant

The little finger, third finger and the other half of the middle finger in the upper part of the palm, is called the Active Unconscious quadrant. This inner active area is concerned with close personal relationships and our sexuality.

Third Area – The Passive Conscious Quadrant

The area of the thumb crossing to the middle of the palm and then straight down to the wrist in the lowest part of the palm, is known as the Passive Conscious quadrant. This outer passive area is connected to spiritual energy and creative potential which, if harnessed, improves the world for mankind.

Fourth Area – The Passive Unconscious Quadrant

The area from the middle of the palm low down and over to the outer edge is called the Passive Unconscious quadrant. This is the inner passive area and presents a direct relationship with the subconscious, revealing our deep desires on a personal level.

The Plain of Mars

The space that is known as the Plain of Mars is the middle strip of the palm. This space starts below the Head Line. It must include both the upper and lower Mounts of Mars, which are on opposite sides of the palms. This section tapers off as it moves down towards the wrist, ending in a point. The Plain forms a triangle in the palm similar to an inverted pyramid.

The Mars Mounts show our active and passive courage. The hollow of the palm is connected to our physical constitution, as revealed in Chapter 6. It reveals our energy capacity and our resilience. This centre of the palm is an extremely excitable spot, since the nerve fibres radiate in all directions. The thicker the palm beneath the hollow is, the stronger the person will be. The thickness of the centre point can also give us an insight into how fortunate we may be in life. I call this 'The Bowl of Luck'. The thicker it is, the greater the returns.

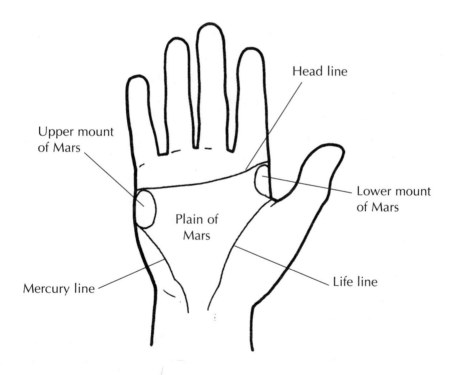

Figure 27: The Plain of Mars

Thin

If the palm beneath the hollow is thin then it just means that liberties cannot be taken with the health, which will not be the best without due care. They are usually extremely sensitive and would rather take the easy road out. Dislikes fighting or quarrelling.

Thick

When the hollow is only slight, the person has no fear of standing up for their rights. They love a good argument because they are never threatened by it. Never seems to be ill, and if they are it does not seem to concern them.

Hollowless

No indentation at all reflects the insensitive. Quite hard by nature. No time for other people's illness as they are personally never ill. If they do by chance become unwell then *their* illness is proper and for-real, whereas yours or the other person's, in their eyes, never is.

The Quadrangle

There is another space to observe which lies between the Heart and the Head Lines. This space denotes trustworthiness. It is advisable to look at this area before you confide in a person. This is a great area to look at if you are employing someone as it shows their ability to be loyal to the cause. When the space has lots of fine lines running all over it show a very nervous disposition and a leaning towards irritability. This is the are where the 'Croix Mystique' can be seen. It can usually be found under the finger of Saturn. Being placed here indicates the person is using their psychic ability. Under any other finger it shows that there is talent but they are not ready to use it yet. When the mystic cross seems badly formed is shows a tendency for disappointment in life. Another marking to look out for in this space is the star, this is a very fortunate sign to have as it shows trustworthiness par excellence as well as the ability to gain success in their lives particularly financially.

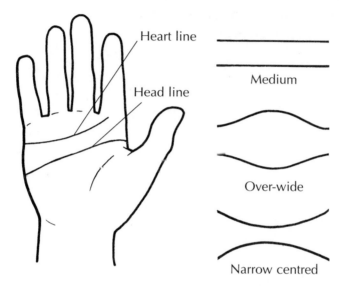

Figure 28: The Quadrangle

Medium-Wide Quadrangle

This is when the space is the same width all along. The person's character will be even tempered and can be relied upon. Faithful in all endeavours. Able to make sound judgements and give good, solid advice. Very discreet.

Overly-Wide Quadrangle

If the space in the middle bulges out so that it becomes overwide in a person's hand you will know that it is best not to divulge your secrets unless you don't mind them being spread about town. It is not that they mean to do this out of any malice or deliberately; it's just that they cannot hold their tongue.

Narrow-Centred Quadrangle

If this space is wider at both ends and narrower in the middle of the palm, giving the appearance of an hour-glass, then it shows a very cautious nature. Can be a little harsh in their judgement towards people. Nonetheless you can trust this person with your secrets – they would rather die than betray a confidence.

NINETEEN

HAND
Speaking

Shaking Hands

Another very simple and sometimes pleasant method of character analysis, is that of shaking another person's hands. Shaking hands forms a cross – the ankh of covenant and a pledge. When we greet someone, in particular socially, the hands engage each other to signify acknowledgement and respect. A person may have given information by word of mouth about themselves and their intentions, but it is wise to take into account the quality of the handshake.

Firm Handshake
The firm, flexible handshake depicts positive energy, someone who is cheerful and optimistic, a person who believes in integrity. Healthwise it denotes a strong constitution.

Hard Handshake
The hand-crusher has a tendency to dominate. They bulldoze through regardless of the other person. Not interested in the opinions of others. Excellent health, which they usually abuse.

Stiff Handshake
The handshake that feels dry and inflexible shows a nervous, highly-strung individual. Difficult for them to relax, they always seem to be worrying. As they are extremely tense, they appear irritable because their nervous system has suffered.

Weak Hand Shake
When the hand seems soft and delicate, it shows that the person does not like to take on too much responsibility. Inclined to put on weight, as they pursue the delights of life and avoid exercise. Good health unless they have over-indulged.

Limp Handshake

If the hand barely clasps yours, or they merely place their hand still closed into another palm, then there is a reluctance towards physical contact. A tendency to not trust people and to not voice their opinions openly. Can suffer from digestion disorders because of pent-up feelings.

Healing Hands

The hands are one of the most symbolically expressive members of the body. They are a tremendous tool and can be put to use in many areas, one of these being as an aid for healing. Because the hands signify power, strength and providence they are able to bring forth the blessing of curing the sick and relieving the distressed. It is noted that the 'hand' of God is depicted as 'divine power' and gives spirit protection. The power and presence of God is symbolized as a hand coming from behind a cloud.

Hands have been used since the beginning of time to bring comfort and ease illness. A mother will automatically rub with her hand, a painful part of her child's body to heal the hurt. We do the same when we are distressed or have discomfort – we gently apply our hands to soothe it away. The right hand is considered to be 'active power' and the left hand 'passive power'. In some cultures the left hand was considered thieving and treacherous but in other cultures it was linked to the heart-centre. Both hands are channels of healing as they each have the ability to push troubles away.

Hand Healing Techniques

Anyone can lend a healing hand. Imagine an invisible circle about three inches wide in the centre of each palm, and from this centre a beam of light full of healing energy pours out from it whenever

215

you wish to give someone healing. The hands can either be placed on the body or a little distance away. It depends entirely on what is most comfortable for both of you. The hands used in this way become channels of healing energy.

A simple technique to employ before trying to heal by the 'laying on of hands' is to rub them both together very hard so that friction is felt. You will feel a tingling and a warmth spreading over them. This pulls energy into the hands and makes them ready to pass on this healing vibration. Always remember that there are two circles in the centre of the palm, like orifices that beam out and pass on the hand's healing powers.

Hand Healing Using Colour Vibration

Before you apply healing hands, you may wish to harness the vibrational energy of colour to give an added dimension to the healing. First choose the colour that will be the most appropriate, then lift both of your hands up to your closed eyes and place the palms in front of the eye sockets, about three inches away. Imagine the colour that you have selected beaming down from above into your head and visualize it pouring from your eyes, streaming into the hand's channels-of-healing circles. Leave the palms there for 20 seconds. Immediately place the hands palms down on the area selected for healing.

Below are some colour guides that you may wish to incorporate in your 'hands on' healing. These can be used safely as a healing aid but are not intended to replace medical treatment. If in doubt, consult a doctor beforehand. To seek specialist colour treatment for an individual, a colour therapist must advise (see address at end of book).

Red

Red can be used for blood disorders – low blood pressure and the reproduction area. As it stimulates, it is also used for exhaustion and lethargy. Never use it for heart conditions. Helps stiffness of the joints.

Orange

Orange can be used for gut and kidney problems, tissue and strained muscle damage. Aids grief and relieves shock, fears and phobias. Useful for the menopause. Clears away mucous.

Yellow

Yellow can be used for any digestive or liver complaints. Helps skin problems and disturbances of the nervous system. Relieves constipation. Lifts depression.

Green

Green can be used to calm and heal the heart. Beneficial in cases of claustrophobia. Soothes headache and biliousness. Heals emotion. A tonic for the whole system.

Blue

Blue is a good healer for all children's ailments. Use for sore throats, speech and vocal problems. Relieves stress. Cools inflammation. Soothes stomach ulcers. Lowers high blood pressure.

Indigo

Indigo helps with all areas of the eyes and nose, particularly sinusitis. Helps with lung and chest problems, lumbago, sciatica, migraine, eczema and bruising. Good for backache and insomnia. It is the strongest painkiller of the spectrum.

Purple

Purple is good for any kind of internal inflammation. Can be used for the brain and scalp conditions. Boosts the immune system. Do not use on children or for anyone who is depressed.

Exercise for the Hands

You may be surprised to learn that you carry a lot of tension in your hands. Everyday activities such as household chores, driving, computer input etc, put a lot of stress into the palms and fingers. It is important to keep them as supple as possible whether it be to allow the subtle energies to fully record in the palm or to enable us to hold a client's hand gently yet firmly whilst giving a reading.

Techniques for Healthy Hands

Wrist Circles

Keep the wrist loose and supple. If the wrist is stiff then there will be a blockage to the hands. Circle the wrists slowly in circles. Make six turns in one direction and then six circles the other way. Do this for two minutes a day.

Wrist Shakes

Vigorously shake the hands so that they are heavy and totally relaxed. This also releases any adverse energy that the hands have picked up. Continue to do this for one minute per day.

Finger Rotation

Starting with one thumb, clasp it with the fingers from the other. Gently rotate the thumb in a circle first one way, and then the other way. Proceed to the fingers until all the fingers and thumbs have been worked on from both hands.

Do this five minutes per day.

Palm Massage

Take hold of one hand and place the thumb of the other in the middle of the palm, so that the palm is clasped from both the front and back of the hand. Press the thumb into the middle of the palm and gently rotate in a circle for two minutes each palm. This point stimulates fiery energy into the palm's centre, releasing energy which promotes health and healing.

Hand Clapping

The way we clap our hands shows us how we live our lives. We can learn who we are by the way we clap. Clapping is used to acknowledge ourselves and other people. Some people at a social gathering clap because they are embarrassed not to! They have not learnt that they don't have to if they don't want to! Or, that they don't have to keep on clapping because everyone else does. Clapping reveals four basic characteristic traits, known as hand patterning.

The Rebel

This is the person who claps when nobody else does, or refuses to even if the performance deserves it. They usually leave the theatre whilst the clapping is continuing.

The Conformist

The conformist does just the right amount of clapping with not one clap before or after anyone else. They politely clap and follow the rules.

The Constrainer

They would love to clap but unfortunately nobody else did so they dare not. Their clapping doesn't have any sound because it is depressed – the same as they are. They find it difficult to give or receive acknowledgement.

The Participator

This person would give anyone a round of applause for anything at any time. In the theatre they applaud when the curtain has been down for at least five minutes. The great optimist!

Clapping Conclusion

You have to ask yourself: which kind of applause do I generate? Do you clap one hundred per cent, or are you not even sure what one hundred per cent is? What does participating mean? Clapping makes you part of the whole; it joins the giver and the receiver. If you don't clap with an energy that shows your true acknowledgement of the proceedings that have gone before, then you must look to see if you just sit, watch, and wait as life goes by! By the way we clap we can gain the understanding that we can either have what we want, or understand that we have internal barriers to receiving it.

The Charming Hand

For many centuries, people have carried a charm in the shape of a hand. The hand was a replica of the hand of Fatima, the daughter of Mohammed. The fingers of the hand represented the qualities of hospitality, generosity, strength and goodness. It was believed that anyone who wore this hand charm would take on these virtues, and that it brought in good luck and protection.

You too will begin to discover that the understanding revealed of both our own lives and the lives of others through our skills as palmists, can provide these same qualities of luck and protection as we act upon that which is revealed.

Where do we go from here?

The best way to continue your development is to branch out and meet other people who have the same interest in finding out about palmistry. You may come across difference of opinions and understanding on the subject, but always remember to keep your own counsel and go with what feels right for you. Practice, practice is where you go from here, in all its many forms. Always keep in mind that your hands are the mirror of your soul. In them is written all the information you need to live your life to its fullest. Not only can the hands diagnose, they can also heal. Our hands link the intentions of our heart with the reasoning of our mind. When we become aware of their unconscious languages and messages, we begin to have totally new insights and sources of information about ourselves. We can change our destiny – the power is in our hands.

The best of luck in your new undertaking.

Appendix

Lilian Verner-Bonds is an international author, lecturer, teacher and healer. Her work is widely recognized throughout Europe, Australia and America.

Lilian comes from a remarkable family of clairvoyants and healers – her great-grandmother was a famous psychic and palmist known to the British royal family, and her father used his gift of healing hands to clear conditions doctors had abandoned.

Her own talent for palm reading began in an unusual way – beneath a hail of bombs! As a small child hiding in London bomb shelters during the Blitz the noise often made it impossible to talk, but she found that just by holding a person's hand she could find out all she needed to know.

Initially, her talents were directed into acting and dancing, and by the age of twelve she was appearing in a West End musical. She went on to a successful career in television, on stage and in films. But even with her busy career, she was studying with a developing psychic circle, which she did for seventeen years.

While still on stage she became a member of the Imperial Society of Teachers of Dance. Her interest in movement led her to yoga, and to the development of special balance and movement techniques that she incorporates in her work today. She has studied the Chinese Five Elements and Shiatsu.

Lilian was involved with the British Marriage Guidance Council, the Doctor-Healer Network, and is Vice-president of the International Association for Colour Therapy. She is a qualified Aura-Soma therapist, and regularly advises clinics and commerce as a Colour Scheme Consultant. She frequently appears on television both as a healer and as a phone-in therapist and consultant.

Lilian does three types of one-to-one personal readings:

Palmistry and Colour Relate Reading A general overall insight for the client from birth to the end of their life. This is a two-part reading using both colour lines and palmistry.

Cards, Colour and Palms This is a reading for people who need an immediate, in-depth focus for now and the year ahead. This is also a two-part reading using a special format devised by Lilian over many years.

Postal Reading This is a reading for clients who are unable to see Lilian personally. Special packs of cards are used, such as the unique French palmistry cards. The reading is taped and forwarded to the client by mail.

Individual personal and public palmistry intensive training sessions are also available, as well as courses, lectures and workshops. For courses, private readings and training, postal readings, or to obtain any of Lilian Verner-Bonds' other books, her CD 'Colour Healing', or cassette 'The Healing Rainbow', contact:

The Colour-Bonds Association
137 Hendon Lane
Finchley
London N3 3PR
U.K.
Tel/Fax: 0208 349 3299
Mobile: 07940 349759
Please send S.A.E. for free information.

Other Books by the Same Author

Colour Healing

Colour Healing is an absorbing, life-enhancing book about colours and their healing qualities. It shows how you can appreciate, understand and use colour on every level – physical, mental and emotional – to enhance your well-being and improve your life.

The Healing Power of Colour and Zone Therapy
Lilian Verner-Bonds and Joseph Corvo

This book brings together two powerful healing techniques in a practical guide to healing a wide range of disorders. It includes an A–Z of diseases and ailments commonly dealt with by healers.

New Cosmic Crystals
with Dr Ronald L. Bonewitz

The dimension of colour is seldom explored within the realm of crystal healing. In this book Lilian adds that dimension to the pioneering crystal healing work of Dr Bonewitz.

The Healing Rainbow Audio Cassette

This tape is an original, unique **active process in colour**. It takes you through a colour-oriented meditation, with specially selected music, which is related to your meditation experience. A detailed explanation is give to allow you to interpret for yourself the discoveries you have made during your meditation.